CEREMONIAL UNIFORMS OF THE WORLD

Italy – Cuirassiers of the Guard 1880

CEREMONIAL UNIFORMS OF THE WORLD

JACK CASSIN-SCOTT & JOHN FABB

ARCO PUBLISHING COMPANY, INC.

New York

Library of Congress Cataloging in Publication Data

Cassin-Scott, Jack.
    Ceremonial uniforms of the world.

    Includes index.
    1. Uniforms, Military—History. 1. Fabb, John, joint author.
2. Title.
UC480.C28   1977   355.1'4   77-1811
ISBN 0-668-04279-6

Published 1977 by Arco Publishing Company, Inc.
219 Park Avenue South, New York, N.Y. 10003

Printed in Great Britain

CONTENTS

INTRODUCTION

Professional soldiers came into being from about the thirteenth century. They were highly skilled and trained in the art of war and were available for hire to anybody who could pay their price.

The Swiss formed mercenary units in the fifteenth century, and these were so successful that their services were eagerly sought by rulers of various states. From that time Swiss Guards became integrated as *élite* units in the armies of many countries. The German Lansquenets, also mercenaries, were founded by the Emperor Maximillian and were the best troops in Europe throughout the sixteenth and seventeenth centuries. These Germans were elaborately dressed, although at that time no official uniforms had come into being. It was not until the end of the seventeenth century that uniforms were established.

From these early times a ruler needed to keep about him a bodyguard of picked troops to guard his person and those of his immediate family. These bodyguards grew in number until a complete army, such as the French Imperial Guard of the First and Second Empires, came into being. The men for these corps were hand-picked, and officers were rewarded by being given commissions in the Guards so that the Guards became an *élite* body, with tremendous *espirit du corps*.

Europe remained the centre of power and dominated Africa and Asia during the period of colonial expansion. The European struggle for control of the American territories continued until, finally, that country itself fought for and gained its own independence. The United States of America remained dormant as a military power until the end of the nineteenth century, when, having subdued the native Indians, they became a rival to the powers of Europe.

As the guardsmen began to take pride in the regimental features and distinctions appertaining to his regiment, the various laces and colours acquired a meaning steeped in the history of the regiment. He was proud to wear his monarch's uniform.

Uniform regulations now began to be introduced, and the military costume became more suitable to the drawing room then the battlefield. The armies became more fashion-conscious. A helmet worn by the Russians was soon observed and adopted by other nations, and could be seen in Prussia or Denmark. The light cavalry fur-crested helmet of France was soon also worn by the Austrian, Württemberg and Bavarian armies.

The exotic military uniforms designed after the Napoleonic War lasted until the Crimean War of 1854, the first major conflict in Europe since 1815.

The conditions of modern warfare soon caused the disintegration of these ornate military fineries which had been inflicted on the soldier. The troops fought in the undress uniform and soft caps. The French uniforms appeared to be very comfortable at this time, with a small shako and a tunic reaching above the knees, full in the skirt and sleeves, following the current fashionable mode for civilians. This was soon adopted by the rest of the European countries, the basic colours showing the national characteristics.

skirt and sleeves, following the current fashionable mode for civilians. This was soon adopted by the rest of the European countries, the basic colours showing the national characteristics.

With the defeat of the French by the Germans in 1871, European nations altered their uniforms, quickly followed by the U.S.A. The army world then presented a Germanic military countenance, with spiked helmets and trousers tucked into gaiters or boots. This was the last time this was to happen on a grand scale. Although complete regiments were dressed in fashions brought from particular countries, such as the Polish lancer and the Hungarian hussar, other items on a smaller scale were added, such as the cloth pad on the shoulder to help keep the rifle in place which originated in Austria, the puttees or cloth bandages wound around the lower leg from Russia and India, and the universal dark green adopted by rifle regiments from the Austrian jäger.

National fashions have now disappeared, except in the guard units which carry on the traditions of armies before the First World War. The new independent states of Africa and Asia have seen the need of *esprit du corps* and have carried on from the Europeans, but with interesting nationalistic fashions.

Garde du Corps units were quite small, those of the French Empire period being the exception. Only in the Austro-Hungarian Empire and the Russian Empire were there numerous Guard regiments. The New Imperial German Empire had several guard regiments, but those that had the honour of guarding their Imperial Majesties were restricted to the Garde du Corps and a palace guard called the Prussian Palace Guard Company, which was composed of non-commissioned officers chosen from the Prussian army specially to guard the palaces at Charlottenburg, Berlin and Potsdam.

Bavaria, the next largest kingdom in the Imperial German Empire, had the ancient Royal Corps of Archers, raised as early as 1580. The distinctive uniform was typical of guards who were eventually only used as decorative and costly features of a ruler's brilliant court.

The kingdom of Saxony employed a Guard Cavalry Regiment, whose helmet depicted a rampant lion gripping a shield bearing the kings monogram. Württemburg employed a Castle Guard similar to that of the Prussian house, wearing a modified form of eighteenth-century dress. These men were all non-commissioned officers of exemplary record.

The Grand Ducal Guard of Hess was stationed at the Palace in Darmstadt wearing a uniform of a more modern appearance. Every duke and prince within the German Empire from the earliest time employed a guard to impress the visitor, rather than for personal protection. Some guards never fired a shot in anger during their service, for example the Westphalian Garde du Corps of King Jerome.

Today the guards are composed of regular fighting units who have the additional honour of guarding the head of state on occasions of ceremony. Exceptions are where a guard is composed of personnel being honoured with a position in a Guard after a life of regular army service. Such is the case in the United Kingdom. Here the sovereign's bodyguard is composed of venerable gentlemen officers with years of faithful service, exemplary records, and a mass of honours and decorations. The Yeomen of the Guard is an equivalent unit, composed of non-commissioned officers with the same sort of service record and achievements. This idea of two Guards, honouring the service rendered by officers and non-commissioned officers, was found in other countries, such as the Austro-Hungarian Empire, with the Noble Archer Guard composed of officers, and the Life Guard Infantry as their counterpart from the other ranks of the army. There were in all six guards attached to the Imperial Austro-Hungarian court, the Hungarian Crown Guard having the duty of protecting the St Stephen Crown of Hungary, the focus of Hungarian patriotism and loyalty. This body continued after the disintegration of the old Austro-Hungarian Empire until the end of the Second World War.

The African states have Guards of honour for their heads of state; some are inherited, such as the President of Ghana's Guard from the British Governor's Guard in the days of the British Empire. In Senegal, Tunisia, Chad and the Ivory Coast the Guards have retained from the past many of the items of dress worn in French Colonial days. Some uniforms are as ancient as many in Europe, such as the Moroccan and Ethiopian Guards.

In the East, the princes of India employed guards wearing the most extravagant uniforms, brilliant colours and jewels. The Maharajah of Cutch was guarded by a regiment wearing pink turbans and uniforms, with white breeches and gilt slippers; they were armed with twelve foot spears painted pink. This was a purely eastern design, but sometimes East and West clashed, such as in the Maharajah of Kashmir's Bodyguard, who wore European helmets and cuirass with otherwise eastern dress. Later, under the influence of the British, the princes of India formed bodyguards who, apart from the turban headdress, wore British army type uniforms.

On the other side of the world, in the Americas, the heritage left by the powers of Europe was incorporated in the uniform designs. In Canada the traditions of the motherland of the old British Empire were carried on by the Foot Guards and the Governor General's Bodyguard. In the United States of America an Honour Guard is used at the White House, on gala occasions, that equals those of Europe for pomp and precision. In Central and South America, European fashion is clearly shown in the exotic and colourful uniforms that formerly existed, as well as in those that are in daily use in the young republics of the continent today. Prussian influence was very strong after the Franco-Prussian War, and military advisors from Germany were used extensively in Bolivia, Chile, Equador and Mexico. The Presidential Guards of today reflect the influence in their ceremonial uniforms, and German influence is also felt in other army units, especially the military academies.

The authors gratefully acknowledge the help of the following persons and institutions: W. Y. Carman; the National Army Museum, London; Colonel W. F. Judd of the Hawaii Air National Guard; J. Hefter, Mexico City; the Company of Military Collectors & Historians (U.S.A.); Captain R. Hollies-Smith and the Parker Gallery, London; and Mr. B. Mollo and Miss Edmunds of the National Army Museum.

THE PLATES AND DESCRIPTIONS

[PLATE I

The Argentine 1904

PRESIDENTIAL GUARD

The Presidential Bodyguard of the Republic of Argentina was constituted in April, 1902 by the then President, General Julio Roca, who had served in the army all his life. As a lieutenant he had fought in the Paraguay war, finishing the campaign with the rank of captain. A few years later, having risen to the rank of colonel, he led an expedition against a revolutionary force under Lopez Jordan, whom he defeated at Naembe. Soon after, he completely routed the insurgents under General Arredondo, for which service he was promoted on the battlefield to the rank of general. At the end of the war he was appointed Minister for War. In 1879 this cuirassier regiment accompanied General Roca in his campaign against the marauding Indians of Rio Negro. This was completed successfully and in the following year Roca was elected President of Argentina. For the regiment's services in these campaigns, it was created the Presidential Guard.

The Presidential Bodyguard of the Republic of Argentina in the first years of the twentieth century presented a very French appearance in their uniforms.

The white metal helmet was ornamented with a brass crest from which flowed a black horse-hair plume. The brass badge plate depicted the arms of Argentina. The white metal cuirass followed the usual European pattern and was bound in brass with brass studs. The epaulettes were dark red with dark red fringing. The officers' epaulettes were of gold, but without a fringe.

The dark blue tunic worn under the cuirass was also worn in undress. This was ornamented with seven rows of black frogging and three rows of brass buttons.

White gauntlet gloves were worn, those of the officers decorated with rows of gold lace. The slashed cuff was crimson with three brass buttons. The breeches that fitted into black leather riding boots were of dark red cloth ornamented with two black stripes each side of the outer seam. In undress the head dress was a kepi, red with a dark blue base, black peak and chin-strap. The short plume at the front was red over yellow. The officers' pattern was slightly different, the body being made of crimson cloth and ornamented in the French style with gold Russian braid. The feather plume was crimson in colour.

The harness was made of tan leather and a small shabraque was used which was of dark blue cloth, edged with two rows of gold lace. In the lower corner were embroidered crossed lances and the crest of Argentina. The sword, slightly curved, was German in pattern; all steel with a plated hilt, a black sword knot and sword belt from a single ring. Officers' swords carried the arms of Argentina in the cartouche of the hilt and also had a gold lace sword knot.

The rank system followed the French pattern and could be recognised on the officers' kepis and sleeves, for example: an ensign – one row of gold cord; second lieutenant – one gold below one of silver; lieutenant – two gold cords; captain – three gold cords; major – four gold cords; lieutenant colonel – five gold cords.

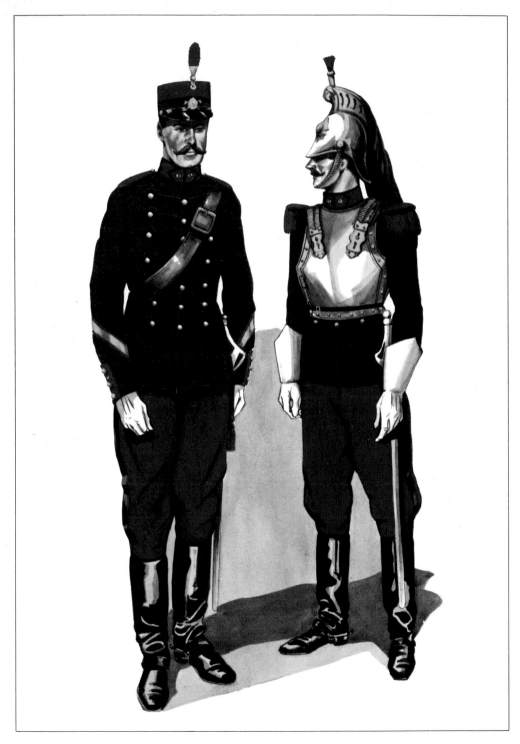

1 Argentine – Presidential Bodyguard 1904

2 Austria – Swiss Guard 1745

PLATE 2]

Austria 1745

SWISS GUARD

The Empress Maria Theresa of Austria was not permitted to head The Holy Roman Empire, the title was therefore offered to her husband, Francis, the third Duc de Lorraine et Bar. Thus he took precedence over his wife as Holy Roman Emperor, but had to give way to her over Austrian affairs. This dynasty, like the other great Catholic ruling families, employed a Volunteer Swiss Guard.

The Swiss Guard attended the great court of Maria Theresa at the Hofburg and at the vast Palace of Schönbrunn, the Guard being placed inside the Palace at the various entrances to the rooms.

The uniform colours incorporated the Hapsburg-Lorraine colours of yellow and black. In gala dress the guardsmen wore armour consisting of a steel helmet with ostrich feather plumes of alternate black and yellow. The helmet was held to the head by means of a leather strap. Around the neck was worn a sixteenth century style ruff. The cuirass was of steel bound in brass and decorated with brass buttons. The shoulder straps were of brass sewn on a red leather lining. The cuirass was secured around the waist by means of a white leather strap with brass buckles and fittings. The jacket was of red cloth with stripes of yellow with a black centre, the upper sleeves puffed out, becoming close fitting on the lower arm. The tan leather gloves had gold embroidered edges. The upper hose had starched linings, allowing the garment a puffed-out appearance, following the fashion of the late sixteenth century. The pattern matched the tunic in being red with stripes of yellow with a black centre. The stockings were white and shoes of black leather were decorated with rosettes of black and yellow. A sword carried from the waist belt in a leather scabbard with brass fittings had a brass hilt.

For ordinary guard duties the basic uniform was the same but with a tricorne hat of black felt with gold lace edging; on the left side a cockade of black and yellow. It was worn with hair or wig dressed white with a white bow; the stockings were red. The ordinary halberd was plain steel, whereas the gala dress pattern had a black head inlaid with silver and a gold Hapsburg-Lorraine coat of arms.

The officers were dressed quite differently, following the more civilian style of dress used by armies at this period. The tricorne hat was bound in gold lace with a gold bow and tassels. The neck-cloth was white, as also was the hair bow. The coat was red, embroidered in gold all down the leading edge and on the pockets. The cuffs were embroidered in a similar way. The waistcoat and breeches were red. The waistsash of black and gold silk had a fringe of the same colours. Officers were armed with a brass-hilted sword and a spontoon with a black steel plate engraved with the coat of arms in gold. The tassel was gold with a black and gold head. White stockings were worn with black shoes which had a rosette of black and gold, the heels being painted red.

[PLATE 3

Austria 1912

FIRST NOBLE ARCHER BODYGUARD

This elite unit was formed in 1763 and served the Imperial family of the Hapsburgs until the fall of the Empire in 1918. The Empress Maria Theresa had decided to form a Bodyguard drawn from her own nationals. Previously this role had been undertaken by mercenaries, including Swiss. The guard known as the Noble Archer Bodyguard was recruited from German-Austrians to complement the Royal Hungarian Guard drawn from the sister nation of the Empire.

The helmet was of white metal bound with gilt brass, and at the front a gilt brass shield depicting the arms of the Hapsburgs surrounded by brass scrolls and filigree. The crest of the helmet supported the double-headed eagle also in gilt brass. From the back of the eagle rose a brass stem from which issued a white plume.

The single-breasted coat was made of scarlet cloth, heavily laced in gold and fastened with gilt brass buttons. The dark blue collar was laced with gold. The cuffs were ornamented in the same pattern as the front of the coat and could just be seen over white gauntlet gloves. The epaulettes were gold and laced with heavy gold bullion fringes. Over the left shoulder was fitted a gold lace pouch belt with gilt chain and pickers, the silver pouch displayed the Imperial arms in gilt brass. The breeches were of white buckskin and were fitted into tall black jackboots. For inclement weather a white cloth cloak with a red stand-and-fall collar was worn.

The sword was the curved cavalry sabre with a gilt hilt and steel scabbard with gilt mountings. The sword knot and tassel were gold. All ranks were commissioned with the rank of captain and above. The corps was commanded by a distinguished marshal, and numbered about forty men in all.

The Noble Archer Guard and the Royal Hungarian Guard were entirely drawn from commissioned officer ranks. There was also a Guard selected from non-commissioned officers of distinction and good record. These formed the Life Guard mounted squadron and the Life Guard infantry company. Their uniform consisted of a black helmet with a peak bound in brass, the badge at the front displaying the Imperial Austrian eagle. The chin scales were of brass. The black falling plume was horse-hair. The tunic was of dark green cloth, double-breasted with a standing collar. The collar was piped in red with a gold laced front. The coat was fastened by eight gilt brass buttons in each row. A black leather waist belt passed between the bottom two buttons, the buckle displaying the Imperial Austrian eagle. The cuffs of the coat were rounded and red in colour. On the shoulders were worn epaulettes with metal crescents, the tops of red cloth. A gold aiguillette hung from the left shoulder and was fastened to the first and third buttons on the right. The cavalry squadron wore the aiguillette on the opposite shoulder. Trousers were green with a red stripe on the outer seam. The cavalry wore white leather breeches and black leather jackboots. These two units protected the immediate vicinity of the Palaces.

3 Austria – First Noble Archer Bodyguard 1912

4 Baden – Garde du Corps 1790

PLATE 4]

Baden 1790

GARDE DU CORPS

The Life Guard at this period consisted of three companies, the Garde du Corps, a cuirassier company and a dragoon company. The uniform was made in the red and yellow livery colours of the Margrave of Baden. The black felt hat was edged in white lace with a white plume issuing from a black rosette. The guardsmen wore a yellow coat lined in red, buttoned back to allow movement in riding. The falling collar was red without lacing and the shoulder knots were of white cord. The right-hand knot had a red and white aiguillette. The coat was edged down the front with broad red and white lace and fastened with hooks and eyes. Over the left shoulder passed a red and white sash and a white leather carbine belt with a white metal snap hook. A red sash fitted around the waist. The breeches were white and fitted into black leather jackboots. The sword had a brass hilt with black leather scabbard, brass mounted. White gauntlet gloves completed the uniform.

Officers in gala dress wore a red coat lined in yellow. The collar was yellow with silver lace embroidery on each side. This was continued on each side of the body of the coat. The cuffs were yellow with two pieces of silver embroidery on the sleeve, similar to that on the coat and collar. The waistcoat was of yellow cloth, fastened with silver buttons. Around the waist passed a silver and red sash. The white breeches fitted into black jackboots. Short white gauntlet gloves were worn.

The officer's sword was similar to that of the guardsman, but of a better quality. The hat was edged in escalloped silver lace, the plume was white.

The Margrave of Baden, Charles Frederick, received the title of Grand Duke from Napoleon, as the reward for submission to the French Empire. He was also forced to supply troops for the Russian front in 1812, of eight thousand men in four regiments of infantry, two regiments of cavalry, one of foot chasseurs, and horse and foot artillery.

In 1819 the Garde du Corps uniform was altered to a Prussian design. In 1835 the body was amalgamated with the Dragoons of the Guard. The 1819 uniform consisted of a black fur-crested Prussian helmet with brass chin scales and a brass helmet plate with a silver star badge. The white coatee was single-breasted with a red standing collar ornamented with two bars of silver lace. The coatee was piped in red with red turnbacks and silver buttons. The epaulettes were of silver metal with red linings and silver buttons. The pouch belt was morocco leather, silver on red. The waist sash was silver with two red lines running through and red and silver tassels. White breeches and tall black boots were used. On less formal occasions grey trousers with double red stripes could be worn.

[PLATE 5

Bavaria 1856

ROYAL CORPS OF ARCHERS

The Electors of Bavaria formed this body in 1669. In the eighteenth century the guard duties became restricted to the court and ceremonies within the palaces until the corps was disbanded in 1918.

The helmet adopted in 1852 was of white metal bound in brass and ornamented with brass studs. A cruciform top of brass supported a holder for a white plume. For gala occasions this was replaced by a sculptured lion in gilt metal. The chin scales were of overlapping brass plates and the bosses depicted the Bavarian crown. On the front of the helmet a gilt brass plate depicted the coat of arms of the Wittelsbachs who were the Electors and later the Kings of Bavaria.

The tunic was Bavarian blue in colour, single-breasted and ornamented with rows of silver frogging and fastened with silver buttons. The standing collar of the same colour was laced all round in silver. The round cuffs were edged in silver lace with ornament similar to that on the tunic front. On each shoulder was a puffed pad of alternate blue and silver bands.

On gala occasions the lion crest was used on the helmet and a white superveste was adopted; this fastened under the arms and on the shoulders with white covered buttons. The lower edge was crimped at the waist, and edged all round in silver. On the chest was embroidered in gold and silver wire the star of the order of St Hubert. This silver star had a white Maltese cross superimposed with a red centre, bearing the motto *In Treue Vast* (Faithful and True).

White breeches were worn with tall black boots (a reminder that this unit was once mounted) and gauntlet gloves of white leather were used with this order of dress. A silver sword belt was worn around the waist, with a depiction of the crown on the buckle. The sword had a silver hilt with gilt grips and was carried in a leather scabbard with silver mountings.

On occasions when the superveste was not worn, a white plume was carried on the helmet. The guards had blue leather crossbelts laced in silver; on the right hip an ammunition pouch edged in silver with a silver crest, and on the left hip a carbine carried in the cavalry manner. Gloves were not worn.

For inclement weather a greatcoat was worn, made of white cloth, double-breasted, with two rows of five silver buttons. The stand-and-fall collar of blue cloth was ornamented at the front with a bar of lace and a button. For walking out a single-breasted tunic of light blue cloth with a standing collar of dark blue cloth and sky blue piping was adopted. This had a single-breasted fastening with silver buttons. The sword belt and sword were used as in full dress. White metal epaulettes were fastened to the shoulder. The cuffs were ornamented with silver lace. Blue trousers with dark blue piping and white gloves completed the uniform.

The glaive carried in gala dress had a blued blade engraved with the Wittelsbach coat of arms on a wooden shaft.

5 Bavaria – Royal Corps of Archers 1856

6 Belgium – Guides du Roi 1850

PLATE 6]

Belgium 1850

GUIDES DU ROI

The black bearskin busby had a loose red bag edged with silver lace and a silver tassel. The white hair plume issued from a silver ornament at the front.

The coatee was of dark green cloth with a plain maroon standing collar. The maroon plastron front ornamented with silver buttons fastened up the centre with hooks and eyes. The turnbacks to the tails were also maroon. The back of the coatee was piped in lancer fashion on the seams and down the back of the sleeves. The epaulettes were of heavy silver lace with silver bullion fringes. An aiguillette was fastened on the left shoulder and made of silver cord. The pouch belt was of plain white leather and the pouch box of black leather with silver mountings. The overalls, fastened under the shoes, were maroon piped with silver lace along the outer seam.

The horse's saddle was covered with a leopard skin edged with white cloth. The shabraque itself was of green cloth to match the uniform, and was edged with broad silver lace. In the lower corners the monogram and crown of King Leopold were embroidered in silver. The valise behind the saddle was of maroon cloth and edged in silver. Holding straps were of black leather. The sword belt was of silver lace and the curved sabre had a stirrup hilt of brass. The scabbard fittings were all steel. The sword knot was of silver lace with a silver bullion tassel.

The uniform was later altered to have a red base to the white plume and the lacing was changed from silver to gold. The green jacket was frogged in the hussar fashion with six rows of brandenburgs, an austrian knot at the end. The red collar was laced all round in gold; epaulettes were not worn, except by officers, who had gold cord epaulettes. The pointed red cuffs were edged in gold lace. The trousers were red with a broad gold stripe down the outer seam. In the late nineteenth century these were leathered on the inside and at the bottoms. The officers wore a pouch belt with chain and pickers.

The Belgian army at the turn of the century was small by European standards. The infantry had four divisions of two or three regiments each. The cavalry consisted of two regiments of Light Dragoons, two regiments of Guides, four lancer regiments, four field artillery and four horse artillery regiments. The army was in the process of re-organisation when the First World War began.

There is also a mounted gendarmerie, used on Royal occasions, who wear a bearskin cap with a white plume on the left-hand side, and a dark blue single-breasted tunic piped red with a standing blue collar edged in white lace. It is fastened by a row of silver buttons. Gold epaulettes with fringes, a white pouch belt, and a white waist belt are worn. On gala occasions the troopers carry lances with a pennant in the national colours. The shabraques are dark blue edged in white, the pistol holsters in three sections. A dark blue cloak lined in scarlet is used in winter. Officers have a fur cover to the shabraque.

[PLATE 7

Bengal 1912

GOVERNOR'S BODYGUARD

The capital of India having been transferred from Bengal to Delhi resulted in Bengal gaining the status of a Presidency, with a Governor who required a Body-guard on the same footing as other Presidencies. This corps was raised in 1912 by Captain R. B. Worgan at Calcutta.

The uniform worn by the British officers was similar to a hussar uniform. The head-dress was the universal white pith helmet with a gilt spike and chin chain which when not in use could be wound around the helmet and fitted to a hook behind the spike. The tunic was of scarlet cloth with a sky-blue standing collar edged with gold lace and a looped gold cord around the inner edge. The shoulder cords were of plaited gold cord on a red cloth with the badges of rank in silver. The jacket was edged all round in gold cord. Across the breast were five rows of gold cord ending in gold caps and drops; these fastened at the breast with gold olivets. The sky-blue cuffs were pointed and edged in gold lace in the form of an austrian knot, and for higher ranks a further row of gold encircled this knot. The back seams were piped in gold cord with a trefoil at the top, two buttons at the waist, and terminating at the bottom of the skirt with a knot. On the right shoulder was worn a gold aiguillette which fastened at the neck. The pouch belt was of gold lace, vandyke pattern, on blue morocco leather with a silver buckle and tip. The chain and pickers were also of silver. The pouch was blue morocco leather with a silver lid, the regimental crest in gilt upon it.

The pantaloons were of white melton cloth and fitted into black leather boots. Silver-plated spurs were used. White gauntlet gloves were an unusual feature of this uniform, for these are not usually associated with hussar dress. The sabretache was edged in gold lace, and embroidered on the sky-blue cloth face was the Imperial crown, Bengal monogram and scroll, 'Bengal' all in gold. The sword had a steel hilt and scabbard. The sword knot was gold with a gold acorn. On dismounted duty the guards wore blue cloth pantaloons with double yellow stripes down the outer seams.

The undress uniform consisted of a blue forage cap with a scarlet band and a single-breasted frock coat of blue cloth, the collar of which was edged with black braid and a figuring of narrow braid with a braided figure on each sleeve, also in black. There were six loops across the chest with rows of olivets. The back and the back skirts were trimmed with black braid with tassels at the waist. The shoulder straps of blue cloth were edged in black braid with the rank badges in gilt metal. The pantaloons were of blue cloth with double yellow stripes. A pouch belt was not worn in this order of dress. The shabraque was of blue cloth embroidered in the corners with the Imperial crown and monogram 'BBG' and the scroll 'Bengal'. The shabraque was edged in a gold lace.

7 Bengal – Governor's Bodyguard 1912

8 Brazil – Presidential Guard 1970

PLATE 8]

Brazil 1970

PRESIDENTIAL GUARD

The last Emperor, Pedro II, was very popular, but his heir, Crown Princess Isabella, and her husband the Comte D'Eu were not. The Brazilians feared the next reign would not be so paternal. On 14 November 1889 the Palace was surrounded by troops and on the following morning they placed the Emperor with his family on board ship to Portugal. No disturbances arose immediately after this act but a series of revolutions followed and it was not for several years that calm was restored.

The cavalry was composed of sixteen regiments, forty battalions of infantry and five regiments of field artillery. Recruitment was voluntary and the numbers made up by ballot, each state having to supply a certain number of men.

The unique helmet of the Presidential Guard of Brazil is of brass; the body has a scaled effect with a winged serpent on the crest. From a conch shell issues a black horse-hair tail and from the left-hand side a red cut-feather plume. The badge in the front is the Brazilian star surrounded by a wreath and ornamental ribbon.

The white coatee has a standing collar of red cloth and is without piping. The coatee is single-breasted and fastened by a row of brass buttons. Metal scaled epaulettes have a gold fringe. The pointed cuffs are red and worn with white gauntlet gloves. The coatee is piped in red down the front and the turnback reveals the red lining. The skirts are ornamented by two brass buttons on the slashing. Over the left shoulder is worn a black leather pouch belt lined in red and decorated on the front with a gilt chain and pickers. Around the waist is wound a red cummerbund and over the top of this item is a black leather sword belt with a brass buckle. The breeches are white and are piped in red along the outer seam. Black leather boots complete the uniform.

The sword has a steel hilt and a red and gold sword knot. The saddle is covered with a South American leopard skin lined and edged in red cloth. Pistol holsters are ornamented in the same fashion. The horse harness is of white leather.

This regiment was the Guard to the Emperor of Brazil, until, unfortunately, the revolution was started by one of its own officers.

[PLATE 9

Brunswick 1828

HUSSAR GUARD

After the War of 1866 in which Brunswick-Hanover fought and lost on the side of Austro-Hungary, the Kingdom of Hanover and the Duchy of Brunswick were acquired by Prussia. In later years the rulers of Prussia had a bad conscience over this, laying the blame on Bismark. Eventually, the German Emperor William II's daughter Victoria, who married Prince Ernest Augustus of Brunswick-Hanover in 1913, was given back the Duchy of Brunswick as a wedding present, including the famous Brunswick crown jewels. The various regiments of Brunswick-Hanover were incorporated into the Prussian army. The hussar regiments' battle honours included the Peninsular War and Waterloo. The Duke of Brunswick who was killed in the Battle of Waterloo was the brother of Queen Caroline of Britain.

The Hussar Guard of the Grand Duke of Brunswick adopted the extravagant fashion that swept through the armies of Europe in the peace that followed the Napoleonic Wars.

The busby made of black fur was rather taller than usual; it also featured a brass bound black peak with brass chin scales. The bag of red cloth, piped in gold, fell loosely to either side. Two swags of twisted gold cord passed round the front of the head-dress. The gilt brass star bore the white horse crest of Brunswick. Below on a separate scroll was the motto: *Nunquam Retrorsum*. The hair plume rose from a gilt cup and was sky-blue with white. The sky-blue dolman had a red collar and gold laced cuffs. The cuffs were pointed, and the front of the jacket heavily laced with nineteen rows of gold cord with gilt buttons in the centre and on the edge. The barrel sash worn round the waist was of sky-blue and silver cord, ending in silver tassels that were looped over the front. The pelisse, slung over the left shoulder, was of sky-blue cloth edged with black fur all round and on the cuffs and was frogged with gold lace and gilt buttons in a similar manner to the dolman. It was lined in red silk.

The tight fitting overalls were of red cloth with a row of gold lace down the outer seam. The sword belt was of silver lace, the slings to the sabretache being the same. The ornamentation of the sabretache, which was of black leather, consisted of the Grand Duke's monogram reversed with the coronet above, both in gilt metal. The all-steel sword had a stirrup hilt with a silver lace sword tassel and strap. The shabraque was of blue cloth with pointed ends bound around the edge with gold lace showing a red line on each side.

9 Brunswick – Hussar Guard 1828

10 Bulgaria – Royal Guard 1912

PLATE 10]

Bulgaria 1912

ROYAL GUARD

Politically Bulgaria was greatly under the influence of Imperial Russia. In military costume, the Bulgarian Royal Guard did display a more nationalistic image. The grey fur cap had white metal chin scales hooked over the plume holding the cockade, the plume in fact being one feather. The badge was a silver star with the king's device in the centre. The cockade was in the national colours of red, green and white.

The hussar tunic was of scarlet cloth with six rows of white frogging. Shoulder cords were white, as was the collar. The tunic was piped all round in white cord, except for the collar, which was edged in gold. The hussar barrel sash was white, the cords and tassels being brought round the right side and hooked over the sash at the front. The breeches were dark blue with a white stripe along the outer seam. Boots were black with a white piped top and tassel. The sword had a steel hilt and stirrup-shaped scabbard with a silver strap and tasseled sword knot.

In undress the uniform was dark blue. The troopers were armed with Mannlicher Magazine rifles. There were at this period twenty-three squadrons of cavalry in the Bulgarian army.

The army was dressed in the Russian style and trained by Russian officers. The infantry wore a green uniform, the collar, the shoulder straps and the piping in the colour of the regiment. A Russian round fur cap was the head-dress. Green breeches were worn, with black boots. In summer an all white uniform was adopted, with a peaked cap of Russian pattern carrying a band of the regimental colours. Officers wore a waist belt of silver with two lines of green and red. Officers of field rank wore a sash of silver with a red and green line that was continued in the tassels that hung on the left side.

The four cavalry regiments used a blue uniform with red standing collar, red cloth shoulder straps and pointed red cuffs. The blue breeches were also piped red. Piping on the seams of the tunic denoted the different regiments: white for the 1st, red for the 2nd, yellow for the 3rd, sky-blue for the 4th. The head-dress was the unusual fur cap with the addition of a metal chin strap of brass and a white plume. These uniforms were worn only on gala occasions, parades and off duty. For all other times a brownish khaki uniform was used which was single-breasted with brass buttons and patch pockets. A Russian peaked cap with a band of the regimental colour was worn in this order of dress. The equipment was black leather.

The King of Bulgaria, Ferdinand I, was a man of great charm and elegance. He collected jewels and was a diplomat. He sided with Germany during the First World War and then abdicated in favour of his son, Boris, who was assassinated by Hitler. Ferdinand's grandson, King Simeon, was forced to flee the country in 1948 when it became part of the new Russian empire.

[PLATE II

Canada 1896

THE GOVERNOR GENERAL'S BODYGUARD

The Canadian Governor General's Bodyguard was formed in 1855 under the title of First Troop Volunteer Militia Cavalry of the County of York. The title of Governor General's Bodyguard for Upper Canada was bestowed in 1865, later, in 1866, Governor General's Bodyguard of Canada. It is now an armoured regiment, having served in both World Wars. Its amalgamation with the Mississauga Horse followed in 1936. The full dress uniform was made very similar to that of the British Royal Horse Guards.

The helmet of white metal was bound around the front and back peak with brass. Around the body seam was a band of laurel leaves continuing up the back seam to the plume. The plume was white horse-hair with a brass rosette in the top. The badge at the front was the arms of Canada on a gilt star, the chin chain of brass backed with black leather.

The tunic was of blue cloth with a standing collar of white, the tunic piped white with eight white metal buttons. The cuffs were pointed with an austrian knot in white cord. The shoulder straps were white and fastened with a white metal button. The back of the coat had two slashes piped in white with three white metal buttons to each. The pantaloons were dark blue with a white stripe on each side of the outer seam. Black leather butcher boots with steel spurs completed the uniform. In addition, over the left shoulder was worn a white leather pouch belt with brass fittings. The pouch was of black leather with a badge of the arms of Canada on a brass star. Around the waist was a white leather belt with a brass snake fitting to accommodate the sword, which was of British cavalry pattern of 1882 – all steel hilt with a pierced Maltese cross and a steel scabbard with two rings each side of the scabbard.

The forage cap was of blue cloth with a white band and button at the top. Officers' forage caps had silver lace and figured silver cord around the buttons. Officers' stable jackets had a white collar and cuffs, with silver cord on the shoulders. The jacket was bound with silver cord and was fastened by five olivets. On duty the pouch belt and sword were worn, and white gloves and a cane were essential items. This uniform was used by the troopers as a walking-out dress and was used with the forage cap or a white pith helmet in campaign during the North West Uprising of 1885.

Straw hats were issued for protection from the sun, but apparently the forage cap was preferred by the Governor General's Horseguards and worn by both officers and troopers. This was the first campaign in which purely Canadian troops were used without aid from Great Britain, the force being transported by rail and then the columns marching through swamp and prairie in three bodies, ending their victorious campaign in Upper Saskatchewan.

In review order the saddle was covered by a black sheepskin.

11 Canada – Governor General's Bodyguard 1896

12 Canada – Grenadier Guards of Canada 1965

PLATE 12]

Canada 1965

GRENADIER GUARDS OF CANADA

The bearskin cap is made from 8½ inches high to a maximum of 10 inches, depending on the height of the wearer. The plume is of white goat hair, 6 inches long, and is fitted into a socket on the left-hand side of the bearskin. The chin strap is made of brass interlocking chains sewn on to a leather lining; this can be altered to fit the wearer.

The tunic is of scarlet cloth with a standing collar of blue cloth piped all round in white. The collar is embroidered in gold wire at the front. The regimental badge of a crown over a maple leaf is superimposed on top of the collar embroidery. The tunic is single-breasted and piped white and is fastened by means of a double row of four gilt brass buttons (eight in all). These carry the design of the regimental crest which is a star with crown above, and in the centre three maple leaves with the motto *A Mare Usque Ad Mare* (From Sea To Sea).

The blue cuffs are round, with gold embroidery around the top, the cuffs slashed with gold embroidery, set in two panels and decorated with four gilt buttons. The skirt flaps are also embroidered in the same pattern and manner and have four gilt buttons. The skirts are lined in white. The shoulder straps are of blue cloth and embroidered in gold all round except the base; they are fastened at the collar with a gilt brass button. The trousers are of blue cloth with a 2 inch wide scarlet stripe. Mounted officers wear overalls of blue cloth with two scarlet stripes fastened under the boots. The spurs are of brass.

The silk waist sash is crimson, with a buckle on the left hip. The pair of crimson tassels are 6 inches long and should hang immediately in the rear of the front sling of the sword belt. On state occasions a waist sash of gold with two crimson lines is worn, with tassels of gold and crimson mixed. The sword belt is of webbing with slings of gold lace lined with red morocco leather. The sword has a half-basket steel hilt with the regimental crest pierced into the cartouche. The black fish-skin grip is bound with silver wire, the blade embossed with devices. The scabbard is of steel, with two bands and two loose rings; the sword knot is of white leather with a gold acorn for undress: gold with a gold acorn for state dress.

The officers' greatcoats are double-breasted of milled Atholl grey cloth, lined with Wellington red, to reach within an inch of the ground. Two rows of gilt buttons ornament the front of the coat in four pairs of two, the pattern the same as that on the scarlet tunic. The deep cuffs turn back 7 inches; the collar is stand-and-fall. There are two pockets – on the left side is a sword slit.

The guardsmen have plain collars except for the collar badges. The shoulder straps are piped white and have the regimental badge at the ends. The slashes on the cuffs and skirt are in white lace. Around the waist is worn a white leather belt with circular brass buckle depicting the regimental crest. The blue trousers have narrow red piping down the outer seam.

[PLATE 13

China 1910

IMPERIAL GUARD

In 1910 the crumbling Chinese Empire, continually attacked by the predatory powers of Europe, was about to fall. The uniforms at this period had changed considerably from only a few years back. Considerable German influence is shown in the cut and design and perhaps the ever-victorious Japanese army also had some influence.

The peaked cap was pearl grey in colour, piped in red with a red band. The brass badge on the front had the Manchu symbol in Chinese characters. The strap was a brown leather fastened by two buttons, one each side of the body of the cap. This strap could be used, and was not false as is usual with a cap of this type.

The single-breasted tunic of pearl grey material was fastened with brass buttons. The low collar had a pair of brass collar badges in the same design as the cap badge. The shoulder straps were of red cloth. On the cuffs were bands of red braid. The breeches were pearl grey and for cavalry the boots were brown leather. The Guard infantry wore puttees and boots, also brown. The cavalry had a similar uniform but with an ammunition bandolier over the shoulder. They were armed with swords carried on leather straps under the tunic. The cavalry also wore a leather waist belt with a brass buckle with two ammunition pouches on each side. Cross-straps over each shoulder supported the waist belt.

Before the Boxer Uprising of 1900 the Chinese and Manchu War Ministries were separate. Now they were united to try and form a modern army, a remarkable feature being that the army was composed of volunteers in only thirteen divisions although thirty-six had been planned, optimistically.

The first uniforms adopted for the army were dark blue in colour for winter dress and khaki for summer. The Guards wore pale grey at all times. Other branches of the service were indicated by the piping and shoulder straps; red for infantry, yellow for artillery, blue for pioneer and brown for commissariat.

Previous to the Boxer rebellion the Imperial Palace Guard wore a type of armour: a steel helmet with a pointed top was decorated with kingfisher feathers. The body armour was in the form of a Brigandine made of two thicknesses of cloth with small iron plates in between them. The outside was of gold brocade edged in black velvet and decorated with gilded studs and round metal plates on the back and breast. The shoulder pieces were of metal in the form of dragons. These dragons had four claws; only the Emperor and Heir Apparent had the right to wear five clawed ones. Apron-like pieces covered the legs, in two pieces to allow for ease of walking and riding. The boots were black silk with thick cord soles. The Guard carried bows and arrows, the armour case of jazerant with black velvet bands top and bottom and a blue fringe. The five ceremonial arrows were of yellow willow with spiral goose feathers.

13 China – Imperial Guard 1910

14 Columbia – Presidential Bodyguard 1928

PLATE 14]

Colombia 1928

PRESIDENTIAL BODYGUARD

This body of troops, created in 1928, is formed of five companies, each representing a different arm of the Colombian army – artillery, cavalry, infantry, engineers and the national guard. It is called the Battalion of the Guard of Honour.

The uniform is copied from the German infantry pattern of pre-1914, owing to the fact that at that time practically all the South American states employed German advisors and instructors. These uniforms still exist for gala occasions and are kept by the military academies in Colombia, Chile, Equador – and at one time in Mexico.

The helmet is of black leather with a front and back peak. The brass binding is only fitted to the front peak and is held at each end by two brass buttons from a circular brass top. A spike is fitted, held by four brass studs. This can be un-screwed to allow a hair plume to be used, such as that worn by the Colombian Military Academy, made of white hair. The helmet plate of brass depicts the coat of arms of Colombia. The black leather chin strap has brass buckles and fittings. The badge also depicts the arms of Colombia; an eagle holding a ribboned shield in its beak and the motto *Liberatad Yorden*.

The tunic is of dark blue cloth, single-breasted and piped down the leading edge in red cloth. The standing collar is of red cloth without piping but orna-mented at each side of the opening by a pair of collar badges. These depict the arm to which the company belongs. The shoulder straps are plain red, each held at the collar by a brass button. The coat is fastened by a single row of six brass buttons. The skirts have a single vent at the back with a slashed pocket each side, these piped in red and ornamented by three brass buttons to each slash. The round-shaped cuffs are red with two brass buttons at the top. The trousers are of blue cloth with a red stripe down the outer seam. In summer white linen trousers have been worn.

Around the waist a white leather belt with a bayonet frog is used with a brass buckle that displays the eagle and shield, arms of the country. Across the left shoulder passes an ammunition bandolier of white leather fitted with four am-munition pouches. The rifle is modern and for guard duties is fitted with a white leather strap.

Colombia gained its independence in 1819 under the national hero Simon Bolivar. At that time it was part of Venezuela and Equador, and did not receive the name Colombia until 1861. A great loss to the country was the breaking away of Panama to become a separate Republic, with, of course, the Canal.

[PLATE 15

Denmark 1970

ROYAL LIFE GUARD

This Guard was formed in 1658 and has been in continuous existence ever since. The red tunic, introduced in 1855, is used on formal occasions such as the king's or queen's birthday, but at other times the blue tunic is worn.

The bearskin cap was introduced in 1803, at the time of the Napoleonic Wars. A sunburst star depicting the coat of arms of Denmark was fitted to the front, together with the cords, tassels and silver chin scales, in the latter half of the nineteenth century. These cords hang down the right-hand side and pass under the right arm up to the back of the neck, where they are arranged around the collar with the tassels at the front.

The standing collar is light blue edged in red piping and the front is ornamented by two bars of silver lace with two silver buttons at the far end. The coat is single-breasted and fastened by a row of eight silver buttons, the leading edge being piped in white cloth. The shoulder straps are of blue cloth and piped in white. At the end nearest the shoulder is a monogram badge of the king, a tradition adopted in 1842. The cuffs are sky blue and pointed in shape, piped white with a bar of silver lace in the centre and two silver buttons at the back. The trousers are sky blue with a wide white stripe along the outer seam. The white leather cross-belts worn by the Guardsmen are connected by a silver cross-belt plate on the right shoulder belt, an item adopted in 1788.

The officer's tunic is similar except for the shoulder rank epaulettes and the bearskin cords which are of gold in place of white. The officer's waist belt is of white leather fastened with a snake fitting, and his sword is carried in a steel scabbard with two rings, the hilt in gilt brass with a silver sword knot.

The blue tunic, worn in place of the red, is without facings but laced in the same manner. This coat is double-breasted and piped red around the collar, cuffs and shoulder straps. The buttons are of white metal. With this uniform is worn the undress cap of light blue decorated with white lace and a tassel on the bearskin. Sky-blue trousers complete this uniform. This was the service dress in 1848 and was worn complete with pack and roll and a waist belt of black leather. A white rifle sling is used on guard duties: this was introduced in 1955. Previously it was of the brown leather type.

15 Denmark – Royal Life Guard 1970

16 Egypt – Mamelukes of the Guard 1810

PLATE 16]

Egypt 1810

MAMELUKES OF THE GUARD

The Mamelukes had existed in Egypt for hundreds of years. They numbered over twenty-five thousand when the Sultan Mohammed Ali lured them into a trap and had them destroyed by his Albanian mercenaries. Napoleon, after the Egyptian Campaign, raised a troop of Mamelukes and these survived until 1815.

The red cloth head-dress was ornamented with a gilt star and crescent badge. The body of the head-dress was enveloped in a white turban held at the front by a gilt clasp. A plume issued from the top of a dark green ball, with a tuft above. The head-dress for officers was further embellished by bands of gold lace around the cap and vertical bands of lace on the body of the head-dress.

The short jacket was of sky-blue cloth with a standing collar of the same colour, this was edged in a gold lace. The upper arms were decorated at the shoulders with austrian knots in gold braid. The pointed cuffs were also sky blue and ornamented with an austrian knot design in gold. The waistcoat was of scarlet cloth edged all round in gold lace and also down the centre. This was fastened around the waist by means of a yellow silk sash with woven bands of green and red. In contemporary pictures troopers are seen to be wearing sky-blue waist-sashes with a tunic of green, laced in the same manner as the officers previously described. The pantaloons were scarlet, very full and baggy, and worn with black boots.

Thrust into the waist sash on the left-hand side was a pistol holster of red leather bound with gold lace and decorated with the star and crescent in gold. Two pistols were usually carried. Over the left shoulder passed a pouch belt of green leather, the pouch box being decorated with the Imperial eagle and crown. The pouch belt had a green leather cover that fastened by means of brass buttons along the face. A curved dagger was often included in the waist sash. The sword, carried on a black leather belt, was curved with a mameluke hilt and gilt crosspiece and held in a black leather scabbard with gilt brass mountings. This sabre varied, especially amongst the officers, according to taste.

The shabraque was generally green cloth with a gold lace edge and a gold and white fringe, an Imperial eagle and crown sometimes ornamenting the corners. Red leather harness with red fringe decoration was further ornamented with the star and crescent. The harness has been observed in brown leather.

In 1863 there still existed Mamelukes of the Guard in the army of the ruler of Egypt. The head-dress was an extremely tall green cap, bound at the base by a white turban. The coat was loose and long, reaching below the knees, and with wide sleeves yellow in colour and edged in red. Under the coat a green shirt was worn, also edged in red. The red trousers were loose and full, and worn with yellow slippers. Around the waist was a red sash. Thrust into this were various daggers and pistols; a sabre was worn at the left hip. A lance was carried, with a steel head and shoe ornamented with a red tuft and two tassels.

[PLATE 17

France 1760

1st SCOTS GUARD COMPANY

The king of France, when in residence at Versailles, was guarded by a force of eleven thousand men. Amongst these was a company of Scots Guards: Catholic volunteers from Scotland, a country that had been a great ally of France.

By the mid eighteenth century the uniform was established in two styles. For state and ceremonial occasions a haqueton of white cloth was worn, heavily embroidered in gold wire with baroque designs of sun bursts, etc. The haqueton had short sleeves, showing the blue tunic which was worn underneath. Red breeches with red stockings and black shoes were worn within the palace, on less formal occasions, and the Guards were armed with a halberd ornamented with gilt studs and a white tassel at the head.

The black felt tricorne hat was edged in white lace with a white cord and button on the left side, securing a white bow. The coat was of blue cloth, the low collar edged in white. The bars of lace were in sets of three with a white metal button on the leading edge, four sets of lace in all. The coat was turned back and fastened for ease of marching. These turnbacks were red in colour. The deep cuffs were of red cloth edged in white with three bars of white lace terminating in a white metal button. The pockets had three points and were edged in white lace and ornamented with three bars of lace of the same design as on the cuffs. At the back of the coat at the waist were three bars of white lace but without buttons. Around the waist was worn a buff belt edged in white. The waistcoat was of red cloth, the edge piped all round in white lace with bars of white lace at each button-hole. The breeches were red as also were the stockings. Over the left shoulder was carried a buff leather belt, piped white, to which was fitted the buff leather ammunition pouch ornamented with the arms of France. The sword and bayonet were carried on the same type of fitting on the waist belt and hung on the left side. The sword had brass fittings. The flintlock musket had a white leather strap.

Sergeants were armed with a spontoon. The uniform was laced like the guardsmen's, but in silver.

Field officers' shabraques were of red cloth edged with two rows of silver lace. The pistol holsters were covered in a similar manner. Officers also wore blue cloaks lined in red.

No one was eligible for service under sixteen years old, and the engagement, to be valid, had to be signed for not less than six years. The barracks of the Guard were so comfortable that the soldiers called them 'Palaces of the army'.

There were four companies of Guards, the first company being Scottish and the other three French. These troops were used in and around the palaces and were called Guards of the Inner Louvre. The Guards outside the Louvre included two regiments of French and Swiss Guards, two companies of musketeers, a company of gendarmes and one of light horse.

17 France – Scots Guard Company 1760

18 France – Cent-Gardes 1860

PLATE 18]

France 1860

CENT-GARDES

Napoleon III, having been created Emperor of the French, formed an Imperial Guard. The first was a regiment of guides in 1852, but on 24 March 1854 a superior body of guardsmen called the Cent-Gardes was created to carry out duties in the palaces and serve the persons of the Imperial family. This regiment had precedence over the other Imperial guard regiments and was in fact listed separately from them. The men were picked for their height and physique. Queen Victoria, on her State visit with Prince Albert to France in 1854, noted in her diary that the Cent-Garde were 'quite splendid'. This corps was very small, consisting of eleven officers and one hundred and thirty-seven guardsmen.

The helmet was made of steel with a brass crest ending in a Medusa head. Above this was a white tuft that issued from a brass cup. From the top of the crest fell a white hair plume that reached halfway down the back. A triangular brass helmet plate depicted the crowned N in a wreath of laurels. The plume was of red feathers, a sky-blue pom-pom at the base. The peak was bound in brass.

The tunic was of sky-blue cloth with a standing collar without piping. For mounted and ceremonial duties the skirts were turned back to display the red lining. The back of the coat had false pockets slashed and piped in red with brass buttons. The cuirass, worn for both mounted and dismounted ceremonial duties, was of steel, ornamented with steel buttons around the edge. The scaled fasteners were of brass. The cuirass was lined in red with a gold piping all round. Epaulettes were of gold cloth with a gold and red fringe – the officers' epaulettes were gold bullion. From the right shoulder hung a red and gold aiguillette that fastened to a hook at the neck of the cuirass. Over the left shoulder passed a white leather pouch belt with brass fittings, on the front an ornamental chain and pickers in brass. The pouch box was of black leather bound in brass, on the lid a brass sunburst with the letter N in the centre. White buckskin breeches with long black jackboots were worn, with steel spurs.

On dismounted duty within the palaces these guards wore a superveste of red cloth piped all round with gold cord; within this was a row of gold lace, in the centre the coat of arms of the Bonapartes. The waist-belt of white leather had a brass buckle with the coat of arms. The sword was carried on white leather sword slings and had a brass three-barred hilt and an all-steel scabbard. Troopers were armed with rifles to which their swords were fitted, an unusual way of using a fusil-lance. Cocked hats were used for walking out, with madder-red trousers.

Other cavalry regiments in the Imperial Guard included curassier regiments of six squadrons each. The guides already mentioned had the same number of squadrons, a regiment of lancers, dragoons and chasseur à cheval. The 2nd cuirassier regiment was eventually re-activated as a carabinier regiment and finally there was a squadron of gendarmerie of the guard.

[PLATE 19

France 1814-15

MOUSQUETAIRE DE LA DEUXIEME COMPAGNIE

The musketeers were formed in 1600 by Henri IV. They were armed with carbines at that time, these being replaced by muskets in 1622 by Louis XII. With the second Restoration in 1815 the mousquetaires were not reformed and disappeared from the French service. Their duties were adopted by the Garde du Corps du Roi which consisted of five companies. The other Royal guards included horse grenadiers of the guard, royal guard lancers, two regiments of cuirassiers of the guard and a regiment of dragoons of the guard. There was also a royal guard hussar regiment and a royal guard horse artillery. These regiments all survived until the Revolution.

The King's Musketeers date back to Louis XIII; they disappeared in the French Revolution, but on the restoration of Louis XVIII in 1814 they were revived.

The classic helmet was of steel, the fittings gilt brass. On the front a gilt disc contained the flamed cross of the Bourbons, with a gilt wreath outside the circle surrounding the badge. The crest was gilt brass with a falling black plume. The white plume on the left-hand side of the helmet had a black base. The gilt chin scales issued from a gilt grenade each side of the helmet, tied under the chin with silver cords. The single-breasted coatee was of red cloth. The red collar was ornamented with two rows of silver lace. The cuffs were also red ornamented with two rows of silver lace, three silver buttons and three bars of vertical silver lace.

The superveste of dark blue cloth was edged with two rows of silver lace, and the centre, front and back, was embroidered the flamed cross. The epaulette was of silver with silver bullions, the top embroidered as the superveste. A silver aiguillette was also worn from the right shoulder. The waist belt was of silver lace with a silver buckle. The cross-belt, also of silver lace, was fitted with a red leather pouch decorated with the cross and French lilies. The heavy cuirassier sword had a gilt hilt, half-basket with the cross design in the cartouche. The scabbard was of steel with gilt brass mountings. The sword knot and strap were silver. The sword belt was of silver lace lined in red leather, the straps ending in a silver tassel.

White breeches fitted into black jackboots and completed the uniform. The shabraque was of red cloth with squared ends and edged all round with a broad silver lace; a narrower silver lace within showed a red light. The corner was embroidered with the flamed cross in silver wire embroidery. The pistol holsters were also covered with red cloth and edged in silver; in the centre was again embroidered the flamed silver cross. The horse harness was black leather.

The uniform so promptly appeared in 1814 that there is some speculation that it was made in London and had been designed by the greatest of all military designers, the Prince Regent of England, later George IV, while Louis XVIII was in exile in London.

19 France – Mousquetaire de la Deuxieme Compagnie 1814–15

20 Germany – 'Liebstandarte Adolf Hitler' 1937

PLATE 20]

Germany 1937

'LIEBSTANDARTE ADOLF HITLER'

Once the Nazi Regime was firmly established, Hitler wished to select a more elite unit to guard himself; with high ranking officials, they were to embody the ideal of the New Germany.

The regiment 'Liebstandarte Adolf Hitler' was formed on 17 March 1933. A combat-ready troop, they guarded Hitler at his various headquarters and also fought throughout the War. Their barracks were at Berlin-Lichterfelde, a former Military Academy.

The black steel helmet, introduced in 1935, for special duties only, was decorated with, on the right side, black runes on a white shield, and on the left a black swastika on a white circle in a red shield. The black tunic had patch breast pockets with centre pleats and buttoned flaps, and pleated side pockets, also with buttoned flaps. The turn-down collar carried rank badges on each side, with only one silver shoulder strap on the right shoulder for officers. Four matt silver buttons fastened down the front of the tunic. From the right shoulder, for officers, hung a silver aiguillette. Around the waist was worn a parade belt with a silver metal buckle depicting the SS eagle and motto. The belt was woven in silver with SS runes and oak leaves alternately. On the upper left arm was a red cloth brassard with two black braids at the edges, and in the centre, on a white circle, the swastika. The cuff title worn on the left lower arm carried, for this guard regiment, a reproduction of the signature of Adolf Hitler. The black breeches were of twill and worn with black boots. A sword, introduced in 1936, and white gloves were worn.

On ceremonial occasions the troops used white leather equipment with white ammunition pouches and belts. The packs were calf skin. On other duties the peaked cap could be worn. This was of black cloth with a black velvet band, the piping in silver for colonels and above, and in white for those below this rank. The chinstrap was of aluminium cord with silver buttons for officers and black leather for other ranks. The badges were the SS eagle with the skull and bones below. In 1937 a white topped cap was introduced for summer wear with a white tunic and white trousers. The greatcoat was of black cloth twill, double-breasted with two rows of five aluminium buttons, the collar piped and fitted with the badge of rank. There were side pockets with flaps and sleeve cuffs. The left-hand sleeve carried the cuff title and the armband. Generals' greatcoats had grey lapels which were worn open.

Officers also wore a mess dress consisting of a black shell jacket with black silk lapels worn open and displaying the rank on the upper lapel. Six matt aluminium buttons with a runic design on them were used and a silver aiguillette was worn on the right shoulder. A white linen waistcoat with lapels and three or four buttons on the outer seam, and a black cape with metal clasps and chain, could be worn with this uniform. The SS eagle appeared on the left side.

[PLATE 21

Ghana 1959

PRESIDENTIAL MOUNTED GUARD

This State on the west coast of Africa, originally a British colony called the Gold Coast, includes the great military kingdom of Ashanti and its redoubtable horsemen of the north.

The last war with the Ashanti occurred in 1900. Even armed with guns there was little the Ashanti warriors could do against Maxim machine guns. The war was over in a matter of months and the king in exile. The war of 1900 had been sparked off by the Governor asking for the Golden Stool to be surrendered to him. This symbol of Ashanti Confederacy is a sacred gold-plated object ensuring the spirit of the Ashanti people. When the war was over, the Stool disappeared: it had been hidden and was kept as a symbol of the continued life of the Ashanti.

The military history of Ghana has mainly centred on the Kingdom of Ashanti which rose in the seventeenth century. By the early nineteenth century the armies were a peaceful force. They had acquired a knowledge of the importance of firearms. Having gold as a natural resource, they were able to purchase guns from the Europeans. The Kingdom absorbed a number of lesser tribes, and with the Northern Emirs levied an annual supply of slaves. The people of the coastal areas were terrified of the Ashantis and were pleased to acquire European, especially British, protection. In 1874 war with the British occurred on a large scale. Unable to stand the accurate fire of the Snider rifles, the capital, Kumasi, surrendered and a peace treaty was signed. There followed a period of peace until 1896 when it was decided that the Ashanti must receive British Protection, for the State had slid back to old ways of bloodshed and human sacrifice.

The uniform of the Presidential Guard was formulated by the Governor during the British period of rule and has been kept on ever since by the Republic. The style is that of the Indian Cavalry. A turban of green has vertical stripes of red. The loose ends of the turban hang down the back and are red in colour with green stripes. On the front is pinned a white metal badge with the arms of Ghana. The long frock coat called a kurta is single-breasted and fastened by six brass buttons. The kurta is green with a plain red collar. Each side of the collar is fitted with a white metal badge depicting the arms of Ghana. White metal shoulder chains protect the shoulders; from the left shoulder a gold aiguillette is fastened to the second button, the metal tags hanging down to the front. Around the waist is worn a red cummerbund, and over this is fitted the white leather sword belt. There is a hook at the waist so that the sword can be fastened in such a way as to allow the wearer to march comfortably when on foot duty. The sword used is the standard British cavalry pattern of 1908, equipped with a gold sword knot. The white breeches fit into black leather riding boots, with white metal spurs. White leather gauntlet gloves are worn.

21 Ghana – Presidential Mounted Guard 1959

22 Greece – King's Evzone Guard 1950

PLATE 22]

Greece 1950

KING'S EVZONE GUARD

In 1824 Greece established a provisional government and five years later Turkey recognised Greek independence.

The Bodyguard dates from the time of Otto of Bavaria's acceptance of the throne of Greece. King Otto lost his throne after a short reign, having sought to rule in an autocratic fashion, and he had given all the best posts in his government to Bavarians. The crown was then offered to Prince William of Denmark, who on acceptance of the throne took the title and name of George I, King of the Hellenes.

The uniforms generally adopted became Danish in style, except for the Guard. The Evzones act as infantry of the line; the ranks for officers are shown by gilt stars, one for a sub-lieutenant, two for a lieutenant, three for a captain first class, four for a captain second class. A major has one gold star with a gold line around the kepi, and a lieutenant-colonel has two gold stars and two gold lines around the kepi.

The army was originally armed with French rifles, but before the First World War took on Austrian Mannlicher magazine rifles. With the French *gras* rifle a sword bayonet was used.

Long ago the Greek mountaineer, like the Scots, adopted a kilt to ease his strides over the rocks. This kilt became the national costume and is part of the uniform worn by the Greek Evzones the King's Battalion. Forty yards of material go into the Evzones' pleated fustanella or kilt, with ten yards of sleeve from the embroidered waistcoat.

The Guards are posted at the Palace in Athens and at Corfu as well as at the Tomb of the Unknown Warrior. Each Sunday morning a platoon of the Guards marches to the Tomb for a changing of the Guard, an honour usually afforded only to the King's person.

At the turn of the century there were eight battalions, each with a distinctive difference in dress. The red cloth beret has a long black tassel that reaches well down the shoulders on the right-hand side. The waistcoat is black, ornamented with a rose of close fitting brass buttons on each side at the front. It is closely embroidered over all with an ornamental design in white. A black leather belt with brass buckle passes around the waist. The white kilt stands well out from the body due to its many layers. The tight fitting hose are white with black garters below the knees. The shoes are black, of a special pattern with large black woollen tufts on the front.

The officer's uniform has the difference of a dark blue shell jacket, single-breasted and fastened with a row of brass buttons. It is ornamented at the edge with two rows of gold russia braid. The collar is red, ornamented with gold lace. A sash of sky-blue and white fits around the waist. Officers wear boots, or red gaiters tied with gold cords with gold tassels.

[PLATE 23

Guatemala 1970

PRESIDENTIAL GUARD

The Republic of Guatemala was established in 1847 after having formed part of the Confederation of Central America for twenty-six years. The country has not been without warfare. It was attacked by an army of combined Honduras and Salvador troops, but succeeded in beating them in 1851. Later that year it was again attacked by Salvador, but eventually the Guatemalans succeeded in winning.

The Polytechnic Army School was formed in 1873 by President Justo Rufino Barrios. He was killed in another battle with the Salvadorans in 1885. A series of these skirmishes occupied Guatemala's army until 1907. In 1917 the country declared war on Germany as an act of sympathy with the United States of America.

The Army School provides on gala occasions a Guard of Honour for the President, formed from the gentlemen cadets. French military influence was apparent although France had just lost the Franco-Prussian War. The uniform on guard duties is as follows. A kepi of red cloth has a broad white band and peak of black leather. The chin strap is of black patent leather fastened by a gilt button on each side of the cap. The plume of parrot feathers is sky-blue with white above. The two cap badges show, above, the arms of Guatemala, and below the badge of the Polytechnic carries a wreath enclosing a five-pointed star of gold.

The dark blue tunic is double-breasted with a standing red collar which is piped all round in black cord. The shoulder straps are plain red cloth fastened by a brass button at the collar. The tunic has two rows of brass buttons, eight in each row. The leading edge is piped in red, and there is false piping on the left-hand edge also. The rounded cuffs are of red cloth. Around the waist is worn a white leather belt with a brass buckle. Over the right shoulder passes a white leather belt to support the black leather ammunition pouch. A white leather belt over the other shoulder supports the bayonet. From the right shoulder strap hangs a gold cord aiguillette which is fastened to the first two buttons on the far left-hand side. The white linen trousers have a black stripe along the outer seams.

The cadets have several uniforms; the combat uniforms are of American pattern. For walking-out dress, the kepi has a red top with gold cord traversing the top. A black band encircles the cap which has the Army School badge. The tunic is similar to the American West Point uniform, grey but with a red standing collar, the same as in gala dress. The patch pockets have brass buttons and the coat is fastened by seven brass buttons. The red trousers have a black stripe each side of the piping seam.

23 Guatemala – Presidential Guard 1970

24 Haiti – Artillery of the Guard 1820

PLATE 24]

Haiti 1820

ARTILLERY OF THE GUARD

The island of Haiti was originally French. After the uprising of the negroes the island became independent. In 1804 their leader Jean-Jacques Dessalines was declared Governor, and the next year, Emperor, under the title Jean-Jacques I. His tyranny and cruelty soon alienated his followers and in 1806 when trying to suppress a revolt, he was assassinated by Henri Christophe, who proclaimed himself King of the northern part of Haiti. Civil War followed and the pride of Henri Christophe caused him to shoot himself rather than be captured. In 1820 General Boyer became Dictator until 1843, when he was expelled from the island. In the following year the people of the eastern part of the island established the Republic of Dominica.

The uniforms of these short-lived monarchs followed the European fashion, and naturally the brilliant uniforms of the French Empire were not ignored. The Artillery of the Guard wore a black leather shako with peak bound in brass. A wide band of gold lace encircled the top of the shako, and two swags of gold twisted cord encircled the head-dress with gold tassels and flounders falling on the right-hand side from a gilt plume holder. At the front centre of the helmet issued a falling plume of white feathers. The badge at the front was in three parts, a crown with crossed cannons below, between the barrels three cannon balls. All these badges were in gilt brass.

The coatee was of dark blue cloth with a standing collar of red edged with broad gold lace with a further row of gold russia below it. The plastron front was worn buttoned back on to the chest, five gilt buttons to each lapel. The coat was fastened at the top near the collar by hooks and eyes. The plastron front and the turnbacks were of white cloth. The open front of the coatee revealed the single-breasted white waistcoat fastened by a row of small gilt buttons. The epaulettes were held to the shoulder by a button at the collar and a gold lace strap over the shoulder through which the epaulettes fitted. The pointed cuffs were red with an elaborate pattern of gold lace above.

The pouch belt was green edged in red, on the centre of the belt at the front was displayed a crown with two crossed cannon barrels, a cannon ball between the barrels, all in gilt. The waist belt was white leather with a gilt buckle displaying a drum with a palm tree, flanked each side by cannons with a trophy of flags behind a motto beneath which read *L'Union Fait la Force*.

The overalls were sky blue and leathered on the inside and at the bottom to give the impression of boots. The overalls were laced with a gold stripe along the outer seam. The spurs were gilt brass. The sword had a brass hilt with a half-basket, also in brass. The sword knot strap and tassel were gold.

[PLATE 25

Hanover 1837

GARDE DU CORPS

The kingdom of Hanover was ruled by the King of England at this time, and it was not until the accession of Queen Victoria, when the Salic Law prevented her from becoming its Sovereign, that the link was severed. The crown was then vested in the younger brother of the late King William IV of Great Britain, Ernest Augustus, 1st Duke of Cumberland.

The black metal helmet had gilt fittings and chin scales. The brass badge depicted the arms of Hanover; the fur crest was black bearskin. The coatee was of dark blue cloth with a red standing collar, ornamented with gold lace. The red cuffs were decorated in a similar manner and had two gilt buttons. The turnbacks were red and the pockets were also piped in red. The cuirass was of brass metal with an edge of white metal, brass studded. In the centre of the cuirass was a silver sunburst with the arms of Hanover above, and separate from this, a small silver crown. The cuirass was lined in red leather and edged in red cloth which was piped red. The scaled fasteners were made of brass. The epaulettes were gold with gilt metal crescent ends and were held in red cloth underneath. The breeches were of sky-blue cloth, with a gold lace stripe down the outer seam. The heavy cavalry sword had a brass hilt with a gold sword knot and tassel. The scabbard was all steel. The shabraque and pistol housings were dark blue edged with gold lace. They were ornamented with the star of the Order of Guelph.

There was also a guard hussar regiment who wore a red shako head-dress laced in gold with a gilt chin scale. The dolman was blue with gold lace froggings. The pelisse was also blue, with black fur, laced in gold. The grey trousers were leathered on the inside and at the bottom.

The Queen's hussar regiment had the same uniform with the difference of silver lace on crimson shakos. The shakos were replaced by fur busbies in 1847. The Garde du Corps altered the helmet at this period to a more Prussian pattern, a metal body with gilt fittings, a star plate with the arms of Hanover and a falling white plume which could be replaced by a spike.

In 1837 the foot guard regimental uniform was altered to the Prussian pattern and in 1849 the Prussian pickelhaube was introduced with the Guard star badge and a falling white plume for gala occasions.

The last king of Hanover was George V, who lost his throne in 1866 to the Prussians. He also had the misfortune to be blind. In 1913 on the wedding of the Kaiser's daughter to the heir to Hanover and Brunswick, the Kaiser returned Brunswick but could not be parted from Hanover. The Hanoverian army was incorporated into the Prussian, and the cavalry renamed King Carl of Rumania's Dragoons (1st Hanovarian) No 9; 2nd Hanovarian Dragoons No 16; Queen Wilhelmina of the Netherlands' Hussars (Hanovarian) No 15; Brunswick Hussars No 17.

25 Hanover – Garde du Corps 1837

26 Hawaii – King's Guard 1886

PLATE 26]

Hawaii 1886

KING'S GUARD

The king of Hawaii was an absolute ruler, with hereditary rulers and governors of islands and village headsmen to dispense his wishes. King Kalakaua I had been elected king in 1874 as a candidate in favour of American annexation and against the Dowager Queen Emma. The King europeanized the army and formed the Royal Guard which numbered fifty-eight men. He also had ideas of obtaining supremacy in the Pacific. However, bribery in an opium concession with which the King's name was connected forced a constitutional government on him. He died in San Francisco in 1891.

Besides the Royal Guard, the army included the Honolulu Rifles, raised in 1857, the Mamalahoa Infantry, the Prince's Own Artillery and the Leleiohoku Guard Cavalry.

The King was succeeded by his sister Liliuokalani, who was overthrown in a revolution in 1895. A short-lived Republic followed, before annexation by the United States of America in 1898. The Americans needed a stronghold and supply depot for the War against Spain.

The military forces of the Hawaiian kingdom included a small guard for the sovereign: the King's Guard. They were dressed in the European fashion, closely following the style then in vogue in the United States of America. The helmet was of cork, covered with fine white drill. The top was ornamented with a brass spike, and a chin chain, also of brass, passed around the body of the helmet from the left side to a hook just behind the spike. At the front was a badge of the king's monogram 'Kalakaua I' with a crown above.

The dark blue tunic was single-breasted, with a row of seven buttons down the front. The stand-up collar was plain. The blue cloth shoulder straps fastened with a button at the collar. A white leather belt with a brass buckle was worn around the waist to carry the bayonet. White gloves and white linen trousers completed the uniform of the Guards.

The officer's tunic differed in being double-breasted with two rows of nine buttons. The collar was edged in gold lace, the sleeve decorated with an austrian knot in gold russia. The waist belt was gold with two lines of blue, with a brass buckle carrying the monarch's monogram. The white linen trousers were of the same pattern as those of the guardsmen. Officers carried a sword and also wore gold laced epaulettes with gold bullion fringes. The guardsmen were equipped with single-shot American Springfield rifles.

[PLATE 27

Hesse-Darmstadt 1750

LIFE GUARDS

This small south German State had a small army which included a Life Guard for the protection of the Landgrave and for Palace duties. The uniform at this period followed the Prussian fashion. The black felt hat was bound round the edge with scalloped silver lace. On the left-hand side a loop of silver cord and a silver button held a black silk bow. A black cord held the hat to the head when riding, fastening with a bow at the back of the neck.

The coat was of blue cloth lined in red material. The shoulder straps were plain blue fastened by a silver button at the collar. The coat was open to reveal the red lining, fastened only at the top with hooks and eyes. Five rows of silver lace ornamented each side of the turnbacks and were held by a silver button on the outer edge. The coat tails were turned back for ease of riding and walking. The turnback cuffs were of red cloth and were decorated in a similar manner to the coat lapels with three rows of silver lace and silver buttons. The pockets of the coat were edged in silver lace and ornamented by three silver buttons. The waistcoat was long, reaching halfway to the knee and was buff in colour, the skirts bound with red and white lace. The upper waistcoat was of the same colour and edged in plain silver lace. Buff breeches that buttoned at the knees fitted into black leather riding boots. Over the right shoulder passed a buff leather pouch belt bound with silver lace. The black leather pouch was fitted with a silver badge bearing the arms of Hesse. Over the left shoulder passed a sash of yellow silk with four rows of silver woven into it, ending in yellow and silver lacing at the right hip. Short gauntlet gloves of buff leather bound in silver lace were worn. The sword was held by a belt under the coat and had a brass hilt and a leather and brass scabbard. The sword knot was silver as was the tassel.

The shabraque was blue, the rounded corners being embroidered with the Hesse lion within a wreath of oak and laurel and other ornamentation with a crown above, the whole in silver. The pistol holsters were in the same manner. A musket carried on the right side completed the armaments.

The companion Life Guard Infantry Regiment, later retitled Life Guard Infantry Regiment (1st Grand Ducal Hessian) Nr 115, was the oldest regiment in the Imperial German army, formed in 1621. The Life Guards had taken part in the Thirty Years War, one of the most savage conflicts in military history, predominantly a religious conflict lasting from 1618 to 1648. In 1820 one regiment became the Electoral Hesse Life Guard Regiment. After defeat by Prussia in 1866 these regiments became part of the Prussian and later of the German Imperial armies.

27 Hesse-Darmstadt – Life Guards 1750

28. Hungary – Life Guards 1913

PLATE 28]

Hungary 1913

LIFE GUARDS

The Hungarian Life Guard served, with their companions the Austrian Noble Archer Guard, in protecting the person of their Emperor, who was also King of Hungary. The regiment was formed in 1760 and when on duty in Vienna was housed in the Palais Trautsohn, originally built for Prince Trautsohn in the eighteenth century. These luxurious surroundings are less surprising when you realise that this corps was formed from the flower of Hungarian nobility. The Hungarian Life Guard shared the honour of being the closest guard to the Emperor with the Anciengarde, the latter being Austro-German. At the fall of the Austro-Hungarian Empire in 1918 such units disappeared, an exception being the Hungarian Crown Guard, whose duty was to guard the St Stephen's Crown, with which the Emperors of Austria were crowned Kings of Hungary. After 1920, when Hungary became a Kingdom again under the Regency of Admiral Horthy, this guard was used in its original capacity once more, but disappeared at the time of the Second World War, as did also the Crown of St Stephen – which is now in the care of the American government awaiting a free Hungary.

The last Emperor of Austria, Charles, who was still Charles IV of Hungary, tried twice to regain his throne. After the last attempt in 1921 he returned to Madeira and died a year later. His son, Archduke Otto, is Pretender to the dual thrones of Austria and Hungary.

The sable busby had a green bag; a white plume issued from a tuft of black feathers, and the twisted silver cords were hooked up on the right-hand side with flounders and tassels.

The hussar tunic was of scarlet cloth cut in the fashion adopted in the latter half of the nineteenth century, with five rows of silver cords with bosses and drops at each end, the centre fastened with a silver olivet. The back seams were piped with silver cords ending in austrian knots. The scarlet collar was edged in silver lace and silver russia braid. The sleeves were ornamented with a silver austrian knot with further embellishments of silver lace according to rank. The barrel sash worn around the waist was of silver and gold cord with silver tassels. Scarlet breeches were embroidered at the thigh with silver austrian knots, embellished according to rank to match the sleeves. Along the outer seam was a row of silver lace and silver russia braid. Across the shoulder on the left was worn a leopard skin, fastened by the paws at the front with a silver oval clasp bearing the arms of the Hapsburgs. The yellow boots had silver tops and bosses with silver spurs.

The undress uniform consisted of the black kepi with gilt fittings and a dark green tunic frogged with five rows of silver cords. The collar was laced around the edge in silver. The cuffs had silver austrian knots. The trousers were dark grey with red stripes on the outer seam. The all-steel sword carried a gold lace sword knot with gold tassel.

[PLATE 29

Hyderabad 1890

AFRICAN GUARDS

Outside the fortified city of Hyderabad, Abdulla Quli Qutb Shah had, in 1676, constructed a huge fortress called Goshamahal Palace. The Hyderabad army had one brigade named after this fortress. The troops, including the African Guards, were garrisoned there.

Hyderabad was the last State to join the Indian Republic.

His Exalted Highness the Nizam of Hyderabad rules over this largest State of India. Hyderabad State had been independent since 1723, having broken away from the Mogul Empire.

Even under British rule the country supported a large army, of over seventeen thousand men, both cavalry and infantry. This included a force called the Hyderabad Contingent which was trained and commanded by British officers, but quite separate from the Nizam's private army, of which the African Guards formed part. The Guards were volunteers from Moslem Africans recruited and sent from that continent.

The Nizam had hoped for independence, but this dream was an impossible one in a land-locked State. The army was prepared to fight and prolonged negotiations carried on for over a year without any agreement being reached. Then in the September of 1948 the Indian army crossed the borders, and after a few days' resistance, the Nizam's army was defeated. It was finally disbanded in 1951, except for one regiment that was integrated into the Indian State Forces.

The red felt tarbush head-dress carried a silver badge on the front – the Nizam's crest with his crown above. The jacket was without buttons and had a standing collar laced all round in silver. The shoulder straps were composed of silver cords looped around a button at the collar. The jacket was curiously rounded at the bottom, rising slightly on the hips. The front was laced in silver, fastening with hooks and eyes; silver lace continued all round the body of the jacket. From the shoulder straps came a further silver lace stripe, a loop of silver lace going from the front to the back stripe. In between the lace on the upper chest was a series of austrian froggings similar to those on a hussar jacket, also in silver. The sleeves were ornamented with a silver austrian knot, but the jacket was without facings, being black throughout. Over the left shoulder passed a silver pouch belt with a silver lion's head, chains and pickers. The pouch itself was silver with a gilt crest upon the lid.

On ceremonial occasions short white gloves were worn. The riding breeches were of plain black cloth. The boots were tall black leather jackboots similar to those used by the British Household Cavalry. The straight-bladed heavy cavalry sword had a steel half-basket hilt with a silver sword strap and tassel. The steel scabbard had two loose rings, and the sword belt was of leather faced with silver lace. Steel spurs were worn.

29 Hyderabad – African Guards 1890

30 India – Governor General's Bodyguard 1910

PLATE 30]

India 1910

GOVERNOR-GENERAL'S BODYGUARD

The first bodyguard squadron was formed in 1773 and some fifty first-class cavalrymen were recruited from the Mogul people.

The trooper shown in the illustration is wearing the uniform which has been worn since 1897. Apart from a few minor changes in detail when India became independent from the British Raj, it has remained unchanged.

The head-dress, a turban or pugri, is dark blue ornamented with gold stripes. A silk band several yards long is worn wound around the head and the kullah, which is a pointed, close-fitting cap, keeps the silk band in place. The fringed tail piece of the band is stiffened and stands up above the head-dress.

The long scarlet frock coat or kurta is double-breasted with seven buttons down either side of the plastron front. The outer edge is piped in dark blue. The cuffs and the collar are dark blue edged in gold lace, the cuff being further ornamented with a double, lancer-pattern, austrian knot. The back of the kurta has a centre vent with pleats either side and ornamented with buttons of regimental pattern, the seams piped in blue. Around the waist is worn a Lancer girdle of yellow with two red stripes, covering the bottom button on the coat.

The plaited shoulder chains are sewn on to blue cloth. The sergeant's chevrons, worn on the right only, are of gold lace edged dark blue. The dress pantaloons are of white cloth, with black enamelled leather Napoleon boots, high in the front and cut away behind. The spurs are of steel. White gauntlet gloves are worn in full dress.

The sword is supported from a white belt with sword slings, which is worn under the lancer girdle. The curved sword fits into a Sam Browne-type frog, the upper scabbard ring being left loose and only the lower locket being fastened. The six foot bamboo lance is fitted with a steel shoe and tip and decorated with the standard red over white lance pennons.

[PLATE 31

Indore (India) 1927

MAHARAJA HOLKAR INFANTRY (MAHESH GUARDS)

The 2nd Guard Regiment, Maharani's Own Guards, Indore, had been raised as Maharani's Own Bodyguard Cavalry, a name used until 1939. These regiments, together with Holkar's Imperial Mounted Escort and a transport corps, make up the Maharajah of Indore's forces.

From the patriotic offers of the Indian States it was decided by the government to form the Imperial Service troops. Some parts of the State army were trained and improved to be able to take their place in the field with the Indian or British army. Practically every State in India was able to supply troops to this standard. The government supplied arms and British officers to train them. There was an inspector general of Imperial service troops to see that the standard was maintained. These troops were able to participate in actions during the Relief of Chitral Tirah, the campaign at Swat, the Mohmand expedition, Somaliland, and the Boxer Uprising in China – where a Victoria Cross was won by a State soldier from Jodhpur.

These troops were drawn from the inhabitants of the States and were not mercenaries, as had been the custom previously, except in Kashmir where the Maharajah was allowed to employ Gurkhas. The Indore forces were used in the First World War: in the Middle East, in France and also in the Sulva Bay landing.

The uniforms of the States were based on British regulations but with Indian innovations. They showed a brilliant and exotic spectacle, the colours blending without clashing.

The State of Indore was founded in 1725 by Maharajah Malhar Rao Holkar and has over one million subjects. The regiment had two companies and was known as the Mahesh Guards. The uniform was of course very British in character, except for the turban. This was blue with a woven gold and blue end hanging down behind the head. The tunic was of scarlet cloth with white collar and cuffs. The collar was edged at the top and front with gold lace, the regimental badge displayed on each side of the collar. The cuffs were pointed and edged in gold lace with russia braid above and below, and an ornamental austrian knot above. The leading edge of the tunic was piped in white cloth. The tunic was fastened by seven gilt brass buttons of regimental design. There were two buttons at the back, at the waist, above the white piped pleats. The gold woven shoulder cords were fastened by a gilt brass button at the collar. A crimson silk sash passed around the waist fastening on the left hip with crimson tassels. The trousers were of blue cloth with a scarlet stripe down the outer seam. These trousers fastened under the boots for officers of field rank.

The sword belt, worn under the tunic, had gold lace sword slings on red morocco leather. The all-steel infantry sword carried a gold and crimson sword knot.

31 Indore (India) – Maharajah Holkar Infantry (Mahesh Guards) 1927

32 Ireland – Irish Guard 1900

PLATE 32]

Ireland 1900

IRISH GUARDS

Queen Victoria decided to form a regiment of Irish Guards in April 1900 in honour of the distinguished service of the Irish troops in the South African War. Irish officers from other regiments were allowed to join. The first colonel was to be Field Marshal Lord Roberts, one of the most famous Victorian Irish soldiers. An Irish Guard regiment had been formed by Charles II. Later when James II abdicated, the Irish Guard served the King of France.

On St Patrick's Day a parade is held during which shamrock is given out to be placed in the men's caps. This ceremony was carried out by all Irish regiments in the British service before the partition of Ireland and the disbandment of the Irish regiments.

The new Irish Guards first appeared as the Irish Guards section of the 1st Guards Mounted Infantry with only one officer and lance sergeant, corporal, drummer and thirty guardsmen. The regimental march is 'St Patrick's Day', the slow march is 'Let Erin remember'. By February 1901 the regiment had a strength of six companies and mounted guard in London for the first time on the 3 March. His Majesty King Edward VII presented the regimental colours on 13 May on Horse Guards Parade, in the same year.

The black bearskin carries on the right side a plume of St Patrick's blue, made of hair for guardsmen and in feathers for sergeants and officers. The guard chain is of brass on a leather lining. The tunic for officers is in scarlet cloth with a blue standing collar piped all round in white. At the front of the collar are two panels of gold embroidery with a silver shamrock superimposed. Ten buttons are grouped in fours, the last two spaced to accommodate the belt or sash. The buttons have the design of a crown and harp. The blue cuffs are round with a white-piped and embroidered slashed panel. In the same pattern is the collar, with four buttons inserted. The skirts at the back of the tunic have slashed panels, embroidered and fitted with four buttons each. There are also two buttons at the waist to support the sash or belt. The shoulder straps are embroidered round the edge in gold, and the rank badges are in the form of the order of St Patrick. A crimson silk sash is worn around the waist; on State occasions one of crimson and gold is used. Before 1902 a white patent-leather sword belt was worn around the waist with a sash over the left shoulder. Mounted officers used a black patent-leather sabre-tache, in the centre of which was the gilt metal badge of the order of St Patrick. Pantaloons and butcher boots were worn with this equipment. This has now changed to blue overalls with a broad red stripe and button under the shoe. The sword is the guards pattern with a white metal half-basket hilt with the star of the order of St Patrick inserted on an all-steel scabbard. The undress cap has a green band with a brass cap badge. The regimental mascot has always been an Irish wolfhound. The first, Brian Boru, was presented to the regiment in 1900.

[PLATE 33

Italy 1880

CUIRASSIERS OF THE GUARD

Umberto I, King of Italy, was now king of a united kingdom, having unified the State by exploiting the astounding passivity of the various Principalities and Duchies. The King married his cousin Margherita, daughter of Ferdinando, Duke of Genoa. Their only son became Victor Emmanuel III. In 1900 Umberto I was assassinated by an anarchist.

The Cuirassiers of the Guard wore a steel helmet edged in brass and decorated with brass studs. The crest was of brass ornamented with an eagle mask at the front. From the crest issued a black horse-hair plume, which fell down to the middle of the back. The plate at the front was in the form of a brass sunburst, with in the centre a silver five-pointed star upon which was shown the monogram of King Umberto I. From the left side issued a white plume from a brass holder above the chin scales, these were of brass on a leather background.

The dark blue cloth tunic was double-breasted with two rows of nine silver buttons. The coat was piped all round in red. The standing collar was red, embroidered in silver wire. The cuffs were red and also embroidered in silver wire similar to that on the collar. The cuirass was of steel, edged in brass and ornamented with brass studs. The shoulder scale fasteners were of brass. On the front of the cuirass was a brass sunburst, in the centre of which was fastened the silver five-pointed star bearing the monogram of King Umberto I. The cuirass was lined in red leather with a border of red, white and red cloth to prevent it rubbing the tunic. On the shoulders were worn silver metal scaled epaulettes with silver crescents. The fringe was of silver bullion. Around the waist the officers wore a sky-blue sash with sky-blue tassels hanging from the left hip. The breeches for gala dress were white and fitted into black jackboots with steel spurs. The gauntlet gloves were white leather. The sword had a half basket hilt of chased steel with a steel scabbard. The sword knot strap and tassel were gold.

In full dress, officers wore sky-blue breeches with a broad red stripe each side of the seam and black knee-length riding boots. The tunic under the cuirass was similar in cut except that the cuffs were plain and the collar ornamented with silver lace and a silver star. No plume was worn in this order of dress. In dismounted gala dress without the cuirass, the gala dress tunic was worn, with the addition of an aiguillette of twisted silver cords that hung from the left epaulette and fastened to the right-hand buttons. The dark blue overalls carried double red stripes on the seams.

The guardsmen had a white-over-red plume, and their epaulettes had white cloth tops with white fringe. The collar was ornamented with two bars of white lace and a white metal star, and the plain blue cuffs were piped red. On guard they carried rifles with fixed bayonets.

The shabraque was of red cloth with pointed ends and edged in a broad silver lace. In the rear corners were embroidered in silver the King's monogram with a crown above. The saddle was covered by a black sheepskin.

33 Italy – Cuirassiers of the Guard 1880

34 Jammu-Kashmir – Maharajah's Bodyguard 1901

PLATE 34]

Jammu-Kashmir 1901

MAHARAJAH'S BODYGUARD

The State of Jammu-Kashmir is in the north of India, bordered by the USSR, China, Afghanistan and Pakistan. The Maharajah of Jammu, Ranjit Singh, obtained Kashmir from the British in 1846 in return for the help given by him in the Sikh Wars; thus a Hindu ruler obtained a Muslim State, which resulted in the Kashmir problem of recent years.

The Maharajah's army was gradually altered from levies to a standing army, and by the last quarter of the nineteenth century the Maharajah Gulab Singh had a standing army of over twenty-two thousand troops, comprising cavalry, artillery and infantry. These troops guarded the northern frontiers, thus relieving the British army in this part of the frontier. Kashmir troops fought in the Chitral campaign and in Gilgit, and later in the First and Second World Wars.

The Kashmir troops have an honourable record of active service; at Chilas in 1893 two hundred and seventy Kashmir troops held thousands of frontier tribesmen at bay for hours, and finally defeated them in a counter attack. In the defence of Chitral the 6th and 7th infantry regiments are particularly remembered. After the partition of India the Kashmir army unfortunately fragmented into various religious groups.

The Bodyguard units were gradually being reclothed in uniforms similar to the Indian army. The old exotic feudatory dress was fast disappearing and it is possible that the Delhi Durbar of 1901 was the last time that these troops were to be seen by many people, both Indian and European.

The Bodyguard of the Maharajah at the Delhi Durbar of 1901 wore a brass helmet with chin chain also of brass. From an ornamental spike was worn a falling plume of red horse-hair.

The long blue coat called an alkalak had a standing collar, without a facing colour. The cuirass was of brass, the edge studded with brass. In the centre a sunburst contained the arms of Jammu-Kashmir. The cuirass was held to the shoulders by means of adjustable chain straps and fastened by a belt around the waist. On the arms there were steel bazu bands, curved steel plates covering the outside of the arm from wrist to elbow and fastened by a narrow hinged plate at the wrist. The dark blue breeches fitted into jackboots of black leather. The guardsmen carried bamboo lances decorated with a red pennon. The horse harness was of white leather.

[PLATE 35

Japan 1890

IMPERIAL GUARD

In 1870 the Japanese Emperor assumed all powers and immediately formed an army on European lines, consisting of twelve thousand men trained by German officers. By 1885 it contained seven divisions, one of which was the Imperial Guard; four regiments of two battalions each. The style of uniforms adopted was, surprisingly, French, even though the advisors had been German and the Emperor modelled himself on the Kaiser.

In gala dress the kepi had a red cloth top ornamented at the quarters with gold russia braid. The front carried the Imperial crest. The plume had a red base with white above. The double-breasted tunic was of blue cloth piped along the leading edge in red. The collar and cuffs were also red – the facing colour of the Imperial Guard. The twisted gold cord shoulder straps were fastened by a button on the collar. The austrian knots on the sleeves increased in number according to rank. Two rows of gilt brass buttons, six in each, adorned the front of the tunic. The waist sash for officers was of gold with two rows of red silk, with tassels of mixed gold and red fringe. The breeches were of dark blue, with a red stripe each side of the outer seam. Black boots completed this uniform.

In undress, the kepi was worn without the plume, with a dark blue tunic having five rows of black mohair frogging with austrian knots to match. Dark blue trousers had a red stripe on the outer seam. Breeches and boots as for full dress could be worn with this uniform. This was very similar to the French pattern then in use.

The sword was European in character but with a longer hilt, the scabbard, of steel, held by a single band and loose ring. The sword belt was of gold lace on red morocco leather and was fastened under the tunic to a web waist belt. The sword knot had a gold lace strap and a gold acorn knot.

In summer an all-white uniform was adopted, a white kepi with a red band and black peak, the Guards badge at the front. The white drill tunic was single-breasted, fastened by five white metal buttons with a plain standing collar. On the breast were two pockets without flaps; two with flaps were at the waist. The rank star was shown on the plain cuffs. Breeches and boots or plain white drill trousers could be worn. The sword was the same pattern as for full dress. Earlier there had been a white pattern tunic cut as the undress tunic with frogged front and austrian knot sleeves, worn with the white topped kepi with a red band. In 1905, after the conclusion of the Russian-Japanese War, two Guard brigades were formed, drawn from the island of Formosa – a place renowned, even at that period, for headhunters. The Japanese had managed to contain these headhunters after bloody fighting on both sides, more savage than had been seen for decades.

35 Japan – Imperial Guard 1890

36 Jordan – Circassian Bodyguard 1947

PLATE 36]

Jordan 1947

CIRCASSIAN BODYGUARD

King Abdullah of Jordan had a Royal Bodyguard, a few of whom remain to this day, of Circassians who had crossed into Jordan after the First World War and offered their services to the King. Most of the higher classes of Circassians were Moslems.

The black cap is made of lambswool and bears, on the front, a silver cap badge in the form of the Jordanian crown. The kaftan is of black cloth, the wide sleeves edged with a broad band of red. On each breast are seven cartridge pipes with a silver stopper and a red cap at the end of each. The kaftan has a 'V' front which reveals the red undertunic with a high plain collar, the only ornamentation being a silver cord front. The kaftan reaches to below the knees from which only the black leather riding boots are visible. A black leather belt decorated with silver mounts supports a kindjal, a knife common to the Caucasus. It has a broad double-edged blade and a very long sharp point. The hilts have broad panels and the grips are usually horn or wood. In the hands of experts it is a very dangerous weapon. The scabbard is of leather and has large silver clasps and lockets. All members of this Guard are formed from those recruited in 1917 – consequently they are rather elderly and the duties of a Royal Bodyguard have been assumed by a mounted Royal Guard; not a Beduin unit, but drawn from the Fellahin inhabitants of Jordan. The shemagh or arab head-dress is red and white, with at the front a silver badge of the Arab Legion. The tunic is of scarlet cloth, double-breasted with two rows of four white metal buttons. White cords across the chest fasten to the buttons. The standing collar of red cloth has dark blue patches on each side ornamented with a button and white cord. The pointed cuffs are dark blue with white piped edges and three white metal buttons. On the shoulders are fitted chains similar to those worn in the Indian army and British cavalry. The riding breeches are dark blue with a red stripe down the outer seam. Black riding boots and white metal spurs are worn and white gauntlets.

The troops are armed with aluminium lances which carry at the head a pennon depicting the colours of Jordan. The officers' uniforms are the same except that rank stars are shown on the shoulder chains. A black leather shoulder belt supports a sword on the left side, or in some orders of dress a revolver holster. In undress a sedara or forage cap can be worn; this is dark blue, piped in red cord, and ornamented with the cap badge of the Arab Legion.

All the horses are greys. The horse harness is of black leather, a red blanket under the brown leather saddle. A throat plume of red ornaments the harness.

[PLATE 37

Korea 1905

EMPEROR'S BOWMEN OF THE GUARD

The Emperor of Korea retained a special Bodyguard of Bowmen. Archery had been held high in esteem by the Koreans from time immemorial. It ranked first amongst the manly sports indulged in by gentlemen, and retained its place in military service until the annexation of Korea by the Japanese. Korean bows were about three feet long and the arrows were made of bamboo. These bowmen were Guardians of the Emperor at the Mulberry Palace in Seoul.

The hats worn by these men were of black gauze. The robes were long, to below the knee, and made of yellow silk material. The sleeves were worn loose. White, tight-fitting trousers and shoes of Chinese fashion were worn.

The Emperor of Korea, Heni Yi, had succeeded in 1864, and in 1897 assumed the title. The country had acknowledged the sovereignty of China until defeated by the Japanese in 1895 when Korea became independent, heavily financed and supported by Japan. The family of Yi had ruled over Korea for over five hundred years. The father of the Emperor who was Regent during his monarchy was corrupt and weakened the Korean government by intrigues after the war between China and Japan. He had the Empress of Korea murdered; the Japanese were implicated and the Emperor became an object of sympathy, particularly from Russia. There came a further struggle between Japan and Russia, ending in complete victory for the Japanese army. By a treaty in August 1910 Japan annexed Korea. The Emperor was deprived of all political power and a Japanese Governor General installed.

The army of Korea had adopted the Japanese uniforms in the French style, with senior officers curiously dressed in uniform but with the Korean hat. Photographs of the Emperor show him wearing a pickelhaube type helmet with a hussar frogged tunic, a waist sash and epaulettes, and a curious conglomeration of several styles of uniform.

37 Korea – Emperor's Bowmen of the Guard 1905

38 Kuwait – Sheik's Bodyguard 1969

PLATE 38]

Kuwait 1969

SHEIK'S BODYGUARD

The Arab Sheikdom situated on the Persian Gulf was under the influence of Great Britain from 1914, but gained independence in 1961. The Sheik's Bodyguard has a distinctive British flavour in the uniform design, but with local Arab differences.

The Arab head-dress is held to the head with a black wool rope. On the front is a white metal badge of the armed forces of Kuwait. The end of the head-dress is tucked through the left shoulder strap. The tunic is of scarlet cloth in the style of the British Brigade of Guards. The standing collar is blue, piped white, with collar badges in white metal. The white metal buttons are arranged in two sets of four. The shoulder straps are blue, piped in white, and from the left-hand side is placed a white cord aiguillette, the points passing through the fourth button. The slashed cuffs are blue and piped in white, ornamented with three white metal buttons, and the slash has a white centre. The white leather belt has a round buckle of white metal. The trousers are dark blue with a red stripe on the outer seam.

The officer's uniform has the same head-dress but the tunic is much more elaborate and is styled like that of the Irish Guards. The coat is of scarlet cloth with a standing collar piped white and embroidered in silver wire at the front. The silver buttons are arranged in two sets of four. The single-breasted coat is piped white down the front. The blue cloth shoulder straps are piped in white cloth and held at the shoulder by a silver button. The cuffs are blue, piped in white with a blue slash also piped white and silver embroidery set in two blocks and ornamented with silver buttons. The skirts are slashed and piped white with the silver embroidery in sets similar to the cuffs slashings. There are two buttons at the waist to support the belt. From the right shoulder hangs a silver twisted cord aiguillette, the silver points passing through the fourth buttonhole. Around the waist officers wear a belt of silver lace with two lines of blue. The circular buckle is silver. The trousers are dark blue cloth with a broad red stripe down the outer seam. The sword, carried on a silver lace sword belt, is of the British Guards pattern with an all-metal hilt. The sword knot, strap and tassel are silver lace.

Non-commissioned officers' rank chevrons are in silver lace on a blue cloth background and have an embroidered silver crown above.

The palace force used on ceremonial occasions wears the Arab head-dress with a dark blue tunic with standing collar, piped white. It is single-breasted and fastened by six white metal buttons and has four patch pockets. The shoulder straps are blue cloth piped white, the cuffs are ornamented with three silver buttons. A white cord aiguillette is worn, like that of the Guards, from the right shoulder. The trousers are plain red. The waist belt is white leather with a white metal buckle, and the rifle strap on guard duties is of white leather.

[PLATE 39

Libya 1951

ROYAL GUARD

After the Second World War, Sayed Mohammed Idris El Senussi became King of Libya. Senussi Sheik were scattered all over Libya, and rose to considerable importance before the First World War, but were driven out by plans of Mussolini's North African Empire. Members fought during the Second World War with the Allies and several served in the Long Range desert group acting as scouts and interpreters. It was after the war that the Sheik Sayed Mohammed Idris El Senussi was proclaimed King of Libya. Before this, Libya had been a part of the Italian Empire, having been conquered in 1911 when Italy declared war on Turkey, nominal holder of the country. The troops landed at Bengasi, which had been subjected to a heavy bombardment by Italian warships. Ten thousand troops were landed, and together the Libyans and Turks suffered four thousand casualties.

By the following year local forces were being raised, with Italian officers, and including Spahis and desert troops mounted on camels. Uniforms were based on Italian styles then prevalent, usually white with a cummerbund. Head-dress could be a turban or a red fez. This situation ended with the Second World War, the defeat of the Italians and the creation of the Kingdom of Libya.

This short lived North African Kingdom had a mounted escort as a bodyguard King Idris. They were dressed in a uniform of European style. A black lambskin cap was held to the head by a white metal chin chain. It had a red bag fastened to the left side by a white metal button, and on the right a looped white cord. The coat was black with a standing collar, also black. The single-breasted coat was fastened by six white metal buttons. The collar badges depicted the crescent and star crest of Libya. The shoulders were protected by chain-mail epaulettes. Around the waist was a red sash with the fringes hanging on the left side. Fastened over the sash was the black leather sword belt with black leather straps and white metal fittings. Over the left shoulder passed a black leather pouch belt with a silver chain and whistle, the pouch was also black leather. Over the left shoulder and under the left arm a red plaited cord passed to fasten onto the third button. On ceremonial duties white gauntlet gloves were worn. The black riding breeches fitted into black leather boots. The sword was all steel with a three-barred hilt of British pattern. The wooden lance had a steel point and shoe with a white leather strap. The pennant was in the Libyan colours of red, black and green.

39 Libya – Royal Guard 1951

40 Mexico – Imperial Palace Guard 1865

PLATE 40]

Mexico 1865

IMPERIAL PALACE GUARD

When the Archduke Maximillian accepted the throne of Mexico, he came to the country with a body of fifty volunteers, all over six foot tall, to form his personal Palace Guard. The uniform of this elite corps of guards was inspired by, and has a great similarity to, various Central European Guards uniforms, although certain details show the Emperor's own individual choice.

The officer with the rank of a captain, shown on the right, is dressed in the Parade uniform. The white metal helmet following the Prussian and Russian fashion carried the armorial eagle, the Mexican eagle holding a serpent in its beak in gilt brass. The helmet was bound round the edges in gilt brass strip. The front plate was a sunray with a badge of the Cross of the Order of the Eagle. The chin-scales of gilt brass were attached to the helmet on both sides by large gilt brass rosettes.

The red tunic worn was Austrian both in colour and appearance, with the exception of the cut-away neckline. The officer's tunic had a wide edging of silver leaf embroidery, and the shoulder pieces were of twisted, plaited silver cord, worn on both shoulders. Aiguillettes, which were worn from the right shoulder, were also of plaited silver cord. The leading edge of the tunic was piped down with silver. The cuff had silver lace and leaf embroidery, edged in a pointed pattern. Around the waist was worn a belt edged in red with buckle of silver bearing the Order of the Eagle design. From this belt hung the sword slings of white leather backed with red. Over this was a wide red sash, fastened at the left side, from which two large silver fringed tassels hung. The breeches were of a white material.

The high black boots fitted with steel spurs followed the pattern favoured by Prussia, Russia and Austria, falling in creases about mid-calf.

The sergeant on the left is wearing the undress uniform. The head-dress was like the French kepi in appearance with a broad green band, edged white around the middle and ornamented on the top and sides in green cord. A white cockade surrounded with red was fastened in the centre. A black leather peak completed the hat.

The rest of the uniform consisted of a long jacket, waistcoat and trousers of civilian fashion. The cut-away collar of the tunic revealed the high white stiff collar and shirt with the black flowing bow tie. The sleeves had short red cuffs edged in white. The wing epaulettes were in white. Red cord aiguillettes hung from the right shoulder. The sword belt with slings was concealed by the waistcoat. The trousers were loose fitting and fastened down under the boots. They were decorated with a wide red stripe down the outside seam. Short white gloves were worn.

[PLATE 41

Modena 1753

MOUNTED BODYGUARD

The State of Modena was ruled by the D'Este family from 1288 until 1860 when the Dukes were expelled and Modena became part of the kingdom of a united Italy. The strategic position of the Duchy involved it in practically all the wars of the Italian Peninsula, neutrality being violated at will by the larger States. Thus Francesco d'Este's prime task was to raise an efficient army capable of maintaining neutrality, if possible. He was never able to obtain neutrality but he did train an army capable of defending the Duchy with some valour. Francesco d'Este, Duke of Modena, succeeded his father in 1737 and had previously served in the Imperial Austrian army. He was greatly interested in army life and developments and also founded a School of Artillery and Fortification in 1757 which survives to this day, housed in the former Ducal Palace in Modena.

During the War of Austrian Succession, the Duke was faithfully served by his mounted bodyguard, which fought on after the army of Modena had been defeated. The guardsmen wore a black felt tricorne hat, laced all round in silver; on the left side a loop of silver cord and a silver button secured a black cockade. The coat was of blue cloth edged all round in silver lace, on each side of the breast five bars of silver lace with pointed ends, secured by a silver button. The slashed pockets were edged in silver lace and had the same lace ornaments as the front of the coat, in a set of three. The gauntlet cuffs were of buff cloth edged on the upper part with silver lace and decorated with three bars of silver lace, buttoned. The waistcoat, also buff, was fastened by a row of silver buttons. The breeches of white buckskin fitted into black leather jackboots with white metal spurs. The shoulder straps of silver cord fastened with a silver button and were unusual at this period; their purpose was to support the buff pouch belt over the left shoulder. This was edged in silver lace and striped across in the same lace. The pouch was black leather. The sword was carried at the waist on the left side and had a silver hilt. The black leather scabbard had white metal mountings, the sword knot was silver with a silver tassel. The shabraque was of blue cloth with squared ends and edged all round in a broad silver lace. The pistol holsters were also blue and edged in a silver lace. The horse harness was black.

On dismounted duties the guardsmen wore white stockings with black shoes.

41 Modena – Mounted Bodyguard 1753

42 Monaco – Palace Guard 1970

PLATE 42]

Monaco 1970

PALACE GUARD

The Principality of Monaco is situated on the Mediterranean coast, bordered by France. The history of the country began in the year 980 when Giballin Grimaldi, a Genoese nobleman, was awarded the Principality for his prowess in ousting the Moorish pirates from Eza, a town near to Monaco and Nice.

In 1817 the Palace Guard was formed by Prince Honore V who had succeeded his father two years previously. He lived extravagantly and was usually away from the Principality. On his death he was succeeded by his brother, Prince Floristan, who managed to lose the towns of Mentone and Roccabruna. They continued as a Republic under the protection of Sardinia until 1860 when they were united with France.

In 1904 the Guard became purely ceremonial and served only at the Royal Palace. The uniform at this time was the plumed helmet, a blue tunic with a standing collar, single-breasted and fastened by a row of nine buttons. The epaulettes and the aiguillettes were the same as those that are used today. The trousers were light blue with a red stripe down the seam on the outside. White gloves completed the uniform.

After the war the open jacket was in vogue, together with white spats; the uniform has a distinct French flavour. A cork helmet is covered with blue cloth. The chin scales of brass can be worn under the chin, or encircle the helmet to fasten at the top near the plume holder. The feather plumes are in the Grimaldi colours of red and white. The tunic is of blue cloth, open in front with a four-button fastening and has four patch pockets. The cuffs are red with, for officers, a piping of gold. The waist belt is of white leather, the brass buckle bearing the Grimaldi arms. From this belt is suspended the bayonet frog, or for officers, the sword. The epaulettes are white with a triple padded end. They are piped in red, each fastened to the shoulder by a brass button. The aiguillette hangs from the left shoulder to fasten under the left lapel of the jacket. The aiguillette is in the Grimaldi colours of red and white. The trousers are light blue in colour with a red stripe down the outer seam. White gaiters fit over the black boots.

In summer a white uniform is adopted. With this is worn a red and white aiguillette and the epaulettes, white leather waist belt and frog, and white gloves. White spats are worn over the black boots in this order of dress. The helmet is of white linen over a cork body with the fittings as on the winter dress helmet. It can be worn with or without the plume. The screw for the plume can be covered by a material covered button. This is similar to the British home service helmet.

[PLATE 43

Montenegro 1900

ROYAL ESCORT

Although a small country, once part of the Turkish Empire, Montenegro was able, by conscripting every male from the age of fourteen, to put in the field an army of over thirty thousand men. The family of Petrovitch Njegos ruled the country from 1697, after liberating it from Turkish rule. The last king was Nicholas I, who by custom walked through his capital with his Royal Escort, making himself accessible to hear grievances from the populace.

Montenegro was a small kingdom between Albania and Serbia and had a Royal Bodyguard dressed more or less in national costume. In 1910 proper uniforms started to be issued, cut in the Russian manner. The Bodyguard, however, appeared in the traditional uniform.

The round black cap bears on the front the brass Royal arms cap badge. The undertunic was white, over this was worn a red sleeveless coat, double-breasted and piped in a yellow worsted lace. Around the waist passed a sash of red, white and black. Stuck through this sash would be a dagger or revolver. The coat of red cloth worn over the waistcoat had sleeves that unbuttoned along the seam so that the arms could be free in hot weather. The coat was without buttons and edged in gold and black and also with black brandenburgs. The white undertunic reached the knees and was worn open to reveal the baggy light blue trousers which were thrust into black boots. The officer's undertunic was green, embroidered in gold. The red waistcoat was ornamented in a similar manner. Blue trousers and boots were worn, of better quality than the men's. Officers carried swords with brass mountings and a revolver or dagger in the sash.

The rest of the Montenegro army was dressed in the Russian style in grey uniforms. The shoulder straps and piping denoted the arm to which they belonged; generals, dark red; infantry, scarlet; machine gun corps, light blue; artillery, yellow; and engineers, green.

The round black cap had a red top and the grey tunic had a stand-and-fall collar for other ranks, single-breasted with cloth shoulder straps, the cuffs plain. Grey breeches and boots were worn.

Officers wore a grey peaked cap of Russian pattern, a grey tunic with standing collar, single-breasted with four patch pockets, grey riding breeches and black leather boots. In gala dress epaulettes were worn and the sword was worn on a belt over the right shoulder.

In 1895 the Tzar of Russia presented the army with 30,000 Berdan rifles, 15,000,000 cartridges and six Gatling machine guns.

In 1916 the Austrians captured Mount Lovtchen and King Nicholas fled the country to Italy. One of his sons supported by the Royalist party proclaimed himself king, but abdicated after a short period. After the Great War the country was included in the new kingdom of Yugoslavia.

43 Montenegro – Royal Escort 1900

44 Morocco – Halbardier of the Guard 1973

PLATE 44]

Morocco 1973

HALBERDIER OF THE GUARD

The Royal Guard can be seen every Friday when the king visits the mosque. They form a route for the king called the Holy Corridor; this ceremony was also enacted by the Sultan of Turkey's Guard before the First World War. The uniform dates from the eighteenth century when the country was ruled by Mulai Ismail.

The King of Morocco's Royal Guard have a completely nationalistic costume, without any apparent foreign influence, except perhaps, the halberd. The head-dress is of cane covered in green material with red and light blue. It is ornamented with the royal crest at the top. The head is swathed in a light blue shemagh. The tunic is of the same colour, with the pockets and the front of the shirt opening edged in gold lace. Around the waist is wrapped a green cummerbund embroidered along the middle with a green and gold design. From the left shoulder hangs a gold and red aiguillette, the only European feature of the uniform; this has red flounders ending in heavy brass acorns. The flounders are decorated with the royal crest: one silver star. From the back of the cummerbund passes a green and gold plaited cord which is fastened at the front, the cord ending in heavy green and gold tassels. The red burnous is worn over the shoulders, the hood piped black. The gauntlets of the white gloves are green, edged in gold lace and decorated with the five-pointed silver star. The pantaloons are a deep blue colour, ornamented at the sides with an Austrian knot design. Black laced boots complete the uniform. The guardsmen are armed with seven-foot halberds with a steel head and shoe.

Of the other two regiments in the Guard Brigade one is mounted and the other on foot. They wear similar uniforms except for the facing colour. The cap is Moroccan in shape, blue in colour with a white diamond on the quarters. Red tunics are worn in winter with a row of five brandenburgs in the facing colour. The collars have red patches at the front. The epaulettes are white with an Austrian knot end and held to the shoulder by a strap and a white metal button. The loose baggy trousers are all red and fit into white gaiters and shoes for the infantry or black riding boots for the cavalry. White leather waist belts are worn with a brass buckle. The infantry have white leather equipment with two white ammunition pouches, one on each side of the buckle. The sleeves have a slashed panel in the facing colour decorated with three white metal buttons. The infantry are armed with rifles and the cavalry with a brass hilted sword of French pattern, and a lance.

In summer both corps wear white uniforms with a red cummerbund, but with the same equipment.

[PLATE 45

Kingdom of Naples 1852

GUARD

This regiment followed the French style of uniform.

The head-dress was a cylindrical shako tapering slightly at the crown, which was embroidered with interwoven circles of silver lace; a single silver lace encircled the top and centre. A gilt brass monogram and crown of Francis II was affixed to the front just above the peak. On top of the shako was a green feather falling plume.

The double-breasted coatee was fastened down the front by hooks and eyes. A high standing collar was piped in red, and so were the sleeves down both sides. The false plastron front of red material was fitted with two rows of white metal buttons. Silver fringed epaulettes were fitted to each shoulder, the one on the left being fastened with silver cap lines, flounders and tassels. A white leather pouch belt was worn over the left shoulder and across the chest and carried a gilt chain and pickers. The silver pouch attached to the back of the belt bore the gilt monogram.

In a steel scabbard was carried the light, curved cavalry sword, with brass two-barred hilt from which hung a silver sword knot. A black leather sword belt was worn round the waist under the tunic.

The shabraque of green cloth edged with red lace was embroidered in silver with the monogram and crown, and over this was the saddle in red scalloped cloth with a black lambskin.

The horse had plain black leather trappings.

45 Kingdom of Naples – Guard 1852

46 Nepal – Foot Guards 1970

PLATE 46]

Nepal 1970

FOOT GUARDS

This small kingdom on the northern borders of India is the home of the Gurkhas, who have been soldiers for the British for over one hundred years. The State has its own forces which include foot guards. These are dressed in a style very similar to the Indian infantry of British Imperial India.

The head-dress worn by all Gurkha regiments in the service of Great Britain has also been adopted by the Nepalese Foot Guards. It is in green cloth, encircled by three bands of white. The top centre has a green wool tuft and at the front is a brass badge of the arms of the Maharajah. The single-breasted tunic is of red cloth fastened by a row of six buttons in brass. The collar is green, piped white. The shoulder straps are red, piped white and have a twisted white cord passing through the end nearest the sleeve. A narrow plastron of green at the leading edge of the tunic ends at the waist. The cuffs are slashed, green in colour, the slashes piped in white with a decoration of three brass buttons. The waist belt is of brown leather, with ammunition pouches each side of the buckle. The trousers are of dark green cloth with a red stripe down the outer seam. The rifle has a white leather strap for ceremonial occasions.

There is also a mounted guard regiment. This corps wears the turban as a head-dress. It is dark blue with the ends woven in vertical stripes of white and a lighter blue. The tunic is red with an unusual wrap-over fastening. The standing collar is dark blue piped in white cloth, the shoulders are covered with chain epaulettes on a dark blue background. The wrap-over tunic is edged in a broad gold lace with the point near the collar decorated with an austrian knot. The cuffs are dark blue and pointed, edged in gold cord forming an austrian knot at the points. The breeches are white cord and worn with dark blue puttees and black boots. The guardsmen wear a brown leather waist belt with a brass buckle and shoulder strap over the right arm. They are armed with a sword of the British cavalry type and this is carried on the saddle. They also carry a lance which has a pennant of red over blue, the national colours of Nepal.

The mounted uniform appears to have been influenced by the Nepal Escort, a small corps used by the British resident or minister plenipotentiary before the independence of India in 1947.

As with the State of Kashmir, the ruler of Nepal is not a Gurkha, but an Indian Rajput, that race having conquered the country in the late eighteenth century. A war with the British in 1814 ended with a peace unbroken since that time. A steady stream of Gurkhas enters the British army.

[PLATE 47

Netherlands 1752

FOOT GUARDS

The grenadier mitre cap was embroidered with the House of Orange coat of arms on scarlet cloth, with at the lower point a red and white wool tuft. The coat for fusilier and grenadier of the guard was the same, with red facings. The collar at this period was turned down, and the coat was piped all round in white, as were the button holes. The coat was lined throughout in red and the skirts were buttoned back to display the lining and also facilitate easy marching. In later years the turnbacks were to become permanent. The large cuffs, themselves turnbacks of the sleeves, were also piped round the edge with white tape, as were the button slashes. The waistcoat was long and cut square, fastened with white metal buttons and secured by a waist belt, which also supported the short hanger or sword. An unusual feature was the colour of the sword knot, it being orange instead of the usual white. White breeches fitted into tall white gaiters that buttoned up the side and fastened under the shoes. Fusiliers wore a tricorne hat edged in white lace, a black bow on the left side. A black leather pouch worn on the right hip was supported by a white leather belt over the left shoulder.

Pioneers of the Foot Guards wore the same uniform with the following slight differences: a large buff apron and the musket carried by a black leather strap over the right shoulder. The axe had a steel head with a black painted shaft bound each end with brass.

The regiment traces its history back to 1599 as the Ernest Casimir of Nassau Regiment. The regiment in later years accompanied William of Orange to England, where it remained until 1702. The colours of the uniforms were then a blue coat with orange facings, but were altered to red about 1750.

When Napoleon captured the country in 1806 the guard uniform was altered completely. A bearskin cap with white cords and tassels and with a white plume on the left-hand side was worn. The chin scales were brass. The white coatee was worn open to reveal the white waistcoat. The plastron front was red ornamented with bars of gold lace with a brass button on the outer edge. The standing red collar had two lace decorations similar to the coatee. The epaulettes had red straps and red wool fringes. White breeches were fitted into white buttoned gaiters; black gaiters were used on service. After the war the uniform was altered to dark blue, but the bearskin has been retained ever since.

The present uniform has been altered in cut and style only slightly from that worn a hundred years ago, the bearskin having a seven-pointed brass plate with a silver grenade in the centre and a red plume at the side. The blue tunic is faced with red, the front ornamented with bars of lace showing a red light between. The cuffs have similar ornamentation. The trousers are lighter blue in colour, with red piping on the outer seam. White equipment is worn on ceremonial occasions with a white sling to the rifle.

47 Netherlands – Foot Guards 1752

48 Nigeria – Presidential Mounted Guard 1970

PLATE 48]

Nigeria 1970

PRESIDENTIAL MOUNTED GUARD

Nigeria was the largest British colony in Africa until Independence. The country was little explored until the first half of the nineteenth century. Explorers found a negroid and Berber peoples who had adopted the muslim religion and formed powerful and comparatively civilised kingdoms in the north of the country. These men were exceptional horsemen, and the open country, being mostly desert, is suitable for cavalry in warfare. The horses were traded from the north through the nomadic Sahara muslim tribes.

On the formation of a Presidential Guard of Nigeria, it was decided to adopt certain features of these northern horsemen and the men are drawn mainly from the muslim tribes bordering on the Sahara desert at the northern boundary of Nigeria. There are one hundred and fifty officers and men.

On top of the head is worn a red cap; a shemagh of white linen is worn around this in the form of a turban. It is also wound around the lower face and neck, its cords hanging loosely down the back. The kurtka is of green cloth with a standing collar. The plastron front is piped in red cord and the kurtka is lined throughout in red material. Eight white metal buttons fasten the front of the kurtka. The sleeves are decorated with red cord austrian knots. In review order white leather gauntlet gloves are worn. On the shoulders are seven steel shoulder chains, made of interlocking metal rings as once used by the Indian cavalry to protect the shoulders from sword blows that might sever the arms. This protection was adopted by the British army in India and spread throughout the British Empire.

Around the waist is wound a red cummerbund. White leather breeches with 'V' fronted leather boots and steel spurs are worn. The sword used is the British cavalry pattern of 1908 with a 35-inch blade. It has a steel bowl hilt and a wooden grip and is carried in a steel scabbard with two rings at the mouthpiece that can be attached to a belt or strapped on the saddle. The shabraque is plain red and a throat plume of red hair is used. The saddlery and harness are of brown leather with brass fittings. As a type of horse, greys are preferred. A predominance of green and white in this uniform is due to the fact that these are the national colours of Nigeria and it is therefore fitting that the Presidential Guard should use them. The motto of the army and the State is 'Unity and Faith'.

[PLATE 49

Norway 1970

HIS MAJESTY'S ROYAL GUARD

This regiment was raised in 1856 as part of the king of Sweden and Norway's guards. In 1888 it was transferred to Oslo from Stockholm, then the capital of the united Kingdoms. The creation of a separate kingdom of Norway in 1905 also created a need for a Royal Guard – which this regiment promptly became. The king was elected, the choice falling on Prince Charles of Schleswig-Holstein-Sonderburg-Glucksburg, the younger son of the King of Denmark. The King had taken the name of Haakon VII as a link with the ancient kings of Norway. The Guards' first duty was to attend the new King and Queen at their coronation at Trondheim, the seat of a bishopric and traditional site of Norwegian coronations.

The black head-dress carries on the right side a falling black plume and is held to the head by a leather chin strap. At the front a cockade of the national colours – blue, white and red – is fastened to a white metal badge of the king's monogram, with a crown above. The tunic is of dark blue cloth with a standing collar which is piped in red on the upper edge only. On each side of the collar are two strips of white lace on a sky-blue background. The tunic is single-breasted and piped on the leading edge with red cloth, fastened by eight silver buttons depicting the Norwegian lion grasping an axe. The coat is piped all round the bottom in red. The cuffs are pointed in shape and piped red on the upper edge, ornamented with three pieces of white lace with a silver button at the end of each. There is a further button at the edge of the seam. On the shoulders are fastened green cloth epaulettes with white crescent ends, the fringe also green. From under the left epaulette issues an aiguillette in white cord that fastens to the third button at the front of the tunic. The trousers are dark blue with white shapes each side of the outer seam. The guardsmen wear around the waist a black leather belt with two ammunition pouches on each side, also in black leather. The rifles carry white straps for guard duties.

The officer's uniform is basically the same as the guardsman's. The collars are laced in silver and the aiguillette is made of twisted silver cord, with silver metal tags that hang from the left shoulder (this being, in fact, the opposite way round to the usual way of wearing an aiguillette, with the tags falling from the buttons). Around the waist is worn a crimson silk waist sash with crimson tassels hanging from the left hip. The officer's epaulettes have silver lace tops and a silver crescent end, they do not carry a fringe. The sword has a stirrup hilt in gilt with a gold lace sword knot and tassel. The scabbard is steel. The uniform has changed little in cut since 1860. A green cock feather was introduced for five years in 1864.

49 Norway – His Majesty's Royal Guard 1970

50 Panama – Presidential and National Guard 1970

PLATE 50]

Panama 1970

PRESIDENTIAL GUARD DETACHMENT & NATIONAL GUARD

The Republic of Panama, which occupies the narrowest part of the Central American isthmus, has no armed forces, but during the Second World War a militia force was formed with the assistance of United States officers, called the National Guard. This forms a Guard of Honour on gala occasions for the President of the Republic.

The uniforms are modern and present a style common to the U.S.A. The peaked cap is olive green in colour and has a cap badge of brass depicting a shield with a crossed sword, arrow and lance, a five-pointed star and the scales of justice, above which is a castellated wall with a scroll surrounding the whole, reading 14 DE ABRIL 23 DE DICIEMBRE 1953 TODO POR LA PATRIA. The olive green shirt has patch pockets with shoulder straps. From the left-hand shoulder strap a green and white twisted cord fastens to the right-hand pocket to carry the silver police whistle. The dark green tie is pushed into the shirt which has three brass buttons for fastening. A black leather belt around the waist has a brass buckle and carries on the left hip a ·38 calibre Smith and Wesson revolver, and on the right hip a wooden baton. The trousers fit into lace-up combat boots of the U.S. pattern. American style steel helmets also are worn with a white band wound around the body. In this dress a white leather waist belt is worn with a pouch on each side, supported by white leather braces over the shoulders. The automatic rifle carried has a white leather strap.

There is also a mounted squadron of the National Guard. The uniform differs in having a brown leather shoulder strap over the left shoulder to the waist belt. The revolver is worn on the right-hand side. Dark green riding breeches and black leather riding boots are worn in this order of dress. The uniform shirt has short sleeves with bound ends.

[PLATE 51

Parma 1853

GRENADIERS OF THE GUARD

The Duchy of Parma disappeared after the French Revolution and became first a department and later a part of the kingdom of Italy. After the fall of the Empire the Duchy was given to the ex-Empress Marie-Louise, while the legitimate Duke was given a smaller duchy. The ex-Empress died in 1847. The Duke now returned, but had hardly settled himself before he was swept away by a revolution. His son, Charles III, was one of the most elegant rulers of his time and a collector of uniforms. He set about modernising the army of Parma, and being an admirer of the Prussian military system, he modelled his army's uniforms on theirs; indeed, the uniforms were supplied by that country. Previously the army had been modelled on the Austrian forces, the ex-Empress being Austrian by birth. Naturally the Duke wished this to be altered. He was assassinated in 1854.

The guard's Prussian pickelhaube was of black leather with a square peak bound in brass. A brass cross at the crest had a brass spike which officers could unscrew, replacing it by a plume for gala occasions. The star plate was eight-pointed, in brass. In the centre was the crest of the Bourbons with its three silver lilies. For officers this was in gilt with a blue enamel centre with silver lilies.

The single-breasted Prussian blue tunic had a standing collar of red cloth ornamented with bars of yellow lace, two on each side. The shoulder straps were of plain red and fastened with a brass button at the collar. The sleeves were tight fitting, in accordance with fashion at that time. The round cuffs were red with a slash of the same colour ornamented with three bars of yellow lace similar to those on the collar. Three brass buttons were indented with the Bourbon crest. The skirt of the coat was full, again in accordance with fashion, with two slashes piped red, and ornamented with three brass buttons. Over the left shoulder passed a white leather belt to support the ammunition pouch which was of black leather decorated with a brass Bourbon lily. Another white leather belt over the right shoulder carried the bayonet and a short sword of French pattern. The pale blue trousers were piped red down the outer seam. A brown calfskin pack was carried by means of two white leather shoulder straps.

Officers' tunics had collars ornamented with bars of gold lace, their epaulettes of gilt ornamented with silver Bourbon lilies. The waist sash was of gold with two lines of sky blue through to the fringes of mixed gold and sky blue. Officers carried a Prussian sword with a gold lace sword knot.

51 Parma – Grenadiers of the Guard 1853

52 Peru – Presidential Guard Cuirassiers 1960

PLATE 52]

Peru 1960

PRESIDENTIAL GUARD CUIRASSIERS

The Republic of Peru lies along the Pacific coast of South America. It was liberated by Simon Bolivar in 1824. The country's army was greatly influenced by France before the First World War, and the army dressed in French rather than German costume. Peru declared war on Germany during the First World War, and in the second, though taking no active part, supplied valuable raw materials to the Allies.

The Presidential Guard consists of four squadrons and guards the government palace in Lima, the capital. The uniform is similar to that of a French dragoon of the pre-First World War years. The helmet is of steel, with a brass crest and Medusa head decorating the front, and a triangular brass plate shows a grenade within a wreath of laurel leaves. From the crest falls a black horse-hair plume; from a plume holder on the left side issues a cut feather plume of dark red over white and dark red. These are the national colours of Peru. The chin strap of leather is covered in brass scales.

For summer the tunic is of white linen, single-breasted and fastened by a row of brass buttons; on the shoulders are epaulettes of dark red cloth with a dark red fringe. From the left shoulder hangs a red aiguillette which fastens to the second button. A white leather belt with a brass fastener is worn and on each side is a white leather ammunition pouch. The riding breeches are of dark red cloth with a blue stripe down the outer seam. They fit into black leather riding boots complete with steel spurs.

For winter the tunics are of dark blue cloth with a red standing collar, blue fronted. The tunic is single-breasted, fastened by a row of brass buttons. The cuffs have a red slash ornamented by three brass buttons. On the left shoulder is a red aiguillette, and around the waist a black leather belt with two black leather ammunition pouches. The troopers are armed with automatic rifles and wear white gloves on ceremonial duties, summer and winter. The regiment is designated Cuirassiers of the Guard but the cuirass is not now worn.

Officers wear gold lace epaulettes with gold bullion fringes. The aiguillette is of gold cord. Officers carry a sword from a sword belt worn beneath the tunic. The sword has a three-barred hilt and a steel scabbard with one ring. The sword knot and tassel are gold.

These troops can be seen at their parade ground which faces the Plaza de Armas, a square laid out in 1535 by Francisco Pizarro, the discoverer and conquerer of Peru. The country at the time was in the grip of a civil war between two brothers. Pizarro was enabled by this conflict to subject the country and was later appointed governor with supreme authority.

[PLATE 53

Philippine Islands 1896

GOVERNOR'S BODYGUARD

At this period the Philippine islands constituted a part of the Spanish Empire. The governor was the direct representative of the King of Spain in these islands, and this high office demanded a ceremonial bodyguard to be displayed on suitable occasions.

The white sun helmet was fitted with an ornamental brass spike, while a red leather band passed around the body of the helmet. The badge on the front was of gilt brass. The white single-breasted tunic was fastened by six brass buttons. The rounded cuffs were red and without ornament. The shoulder straps were of plain red cloth piped in yellow. The red collar was fitted with a pair of brass badges. The waist belt of plain leather was fastened by means of a rectangular brass buckle. The belt supported a brass-hilted sword in a black leather scabbard. The hilt was in the style of a court sword with a D-shaped shell guard. The trousers were of dark blue cloth with a broad red stripe along the outer seam. White gloves were worn on ceremonial occasions, and the men carried halberds. These had a wooden shaft with a steel shoe and head, the height being approximately six feet.

The Spanish troops stationed in the Philippines at this period wore a straw hat of jipijapa when on service, in place of the pith helmet used on more formal occasions. The tunic was of a washable white cotton. The collar was green, but the cuffs and trouser stripes and the three cuff flashes were yellow for infantry and white for cavalry. The trousers were of white cotton and worn with black boots. Officers could wear white gloves.

Officers carried a French revolver on the right hip with a lanyard placed around the neck. The officer rank was displayed on the cuffs: three stars and three half-inch lace cuffs for colonel; two stars and two lace cuffs for lieutenant colonel. A major had the same as a lieutenant colonel, but the lace was silver at the top. Officers below this rank wore stars above the cuffs, three for a captain, two for a first lieutenant and one for a sub-lieutenant.

The equipment was of black leather. The waist belt held two ammunition pouches on each side of the buckle, straps over the shoulders supporting them. A bayonet was carried on the left side and a blanket roll was worn over the left shoulder. The weapon carried was an American 1871 model single-shot Remington, a popular weapon because of its durability and strength. In 1892, a five-shot 7 mm Mauser began to replace the Remington. Officers carried both swords and revolvers. The cavalry was armed with the Remington carbine.

The Philippines were lost to the United States of America after the war of 1898 with Spain.

53 Philippine Islands – Governor's Bodyguard 1896

54 Poland – King's Bodyguard 1786

PLATE 54]

Poland 1786

KING'S BODYGUARD

The bodyguard of the last king of Poland, King Stanislas Poniatowski, was dressed in very nationalistic style. The black fur cap had a white pleated top, heavily ornamented with gold lace, and a gold cord encircled the cap, with tassels and flounders on the left side. On the left quarter of the cap was fixed a white plume; below this issued another plume, of yellow feathers. The sleeveless long coat was of cobalt blue edged in gold lace. The plastron front was red, edged in wide ornamental gold lace. The collar was piped red and gold laced with a red line in between. Below dark red sleeve puffs the sleeves were red. The gauntlet gloves were cobalt blue edged with gold lace.

The gold lace epaulettes had gold bullion fringes. The waist sash was heavily embroidered in gold on a red base. The pouch belt was of gold lace with a red centre stripe, the whole mounted on red morocco leather, the chain and pickers silver. The boots were of red leather, and the sword belt silver lace on a red morocco leather lining. The sabre, with a silver stirrup hilt, was in a black leather scabbard with silver mountings. The sword knot was silver with a silver tassel. The troops were also armed with lances of wood with a steel point and shoe; at the head was flown a pennant of black over yellow.

Also in the service of the King was a corps of Royal hussars to perform escort and guard duty. The square topped Polish cap was of black cloth, the lower part covered with a black fur. Around the body of the cap was fitted a gold lace band, and at the front a silver clasp held a white hair plume. The coat reached halfway down the calf of the leg. It was single-breasted and made of scarlet cloth. The standing collar was black, laced all round in gold. On the right shoulder was an epaulette with a gold lace strap and gold bullions. The coat had lapels down to the waist, turned to reveal the black facings, and the plastron was edged in gold lace and ornamented with eight rows of gold lace ending with a gold tassel at the outer edge. The pointed cuffs were black, edged in gold lace. Around the waist passed a silver sash, the tassels arranged on each side of the hips. The riding boots were of buff leather. White short gloves were worn on ceremonial occasions.

A brass baton was carried as a distinction of rank in the Polish service. Its original purpose was to smash open the armour of your adversary.

Before this time, the Polish Guard, when it was united to the Saxon kingdom, wore half armour with a buff coat and a winged Polish helmet, a style then in vogue – and carried on to a much later period by the Russian chevalier guard. There was also a musketeer guard unit; this served only in and around the palaces and wore a much more Western style of uniform, with a scarlet coat trimmed in silver and with buff yellow facings.

[PLATE 55

Portugal 1905

MOUNTED ROYAL GUARD

The Kingdom of Portugal supported a small army before the Revolution of 1910, and this included a Royal mounted guard from which is descended the Republican National Guard of today. The old guards protected the Royal palaces at Lisbon, and the castle Pena at Cintra. The Royal court before the Revolution was magnificient and extravagant and although the King himself had been popular at first, the actions of his government made him, quite undeservedly, unpopular. In October of 1910 an insurrection broke out and the King was obliged to abandon the palace because the fleet, who had mutinied, was beginning to bombard it. A Republic was proclaimed and has remained. There was a Royalist uprising in 1912 which was quelled. Royalist support for Germany during the First World War did little good to the cause. Portugal, in fact, declared war on Germany, and sent to the front a small force of some eight thousand troops, armed and fitted out mainly with British help.

At this time a term of service in the Portuguese army consisted of three years with the colours and five in the reserve, and also four years in the second reserve. The army was organised in twenty-four line infantry and twelve rifle regiments, and ten cavalry regiments including the Royal Mounted Guard. Three artillery regiments, each of four gun batteries, also included fortress and mountain artillery for use on the borders. There was also employed a Municipal Guard of two thousand and two hundred, and lastly a colonial army, used in Africa, of nine thousand troops. Most attention was paid to the Portuguese navy, for expansion of the colonial empire was more important than the possibility of war in the Peninsula with Spain.

The uniform of the Mounted Royal Guard consisted of a helmet bound in brass with a brass chin scale, with a brass spike from which issued a white horsehair plume. The helmet plate of gilt depicted a stand of colours supporting the Royal crown and in the centre, on a silver background, a pair of crossed lances. The blue tunic was decorated with three rows of brass buttons, six in each row. The collar had two rows of gold lace, and the sleeves were decorated with two gold lace chevrons. White gauntlet gloves were sometimes worn. On the shoulders were fitted scaled epaulettes of brass fastened by a strap to the shoulders. On the right shoulder a crimson silk sash was carried, with the tassels hanging at the left hip. On occasions over the left shoulder was fitted a white leather pouch belt. The blue riding breeches fitted into black riding boots. In gala dress, white breeches and knee boots were worn. The sword was carried on two straps, attached to a belt under the tunic. This had a steel hilt, half-basket shape, with an all-steel scabbard. The sword knot was gold lace with a gold tassel end.

55 Portugal – Mounted Royal Guard 1905

56 Prussia – Garde du Corps 1843

PLATE 56]

Prussia 1843

GARDE DU CORPS

The Prussian Garde du Corps at this time wore a uniform which was to remain virtually unchanged until 1918.

The Prussian eagle on the helmet was introduced in 1843. The brass helmet had a stepped peak and was bound in white metal. The star badge was also in white metal and was of the order of the black eagle. The silver eagle could be removed and replaced with a white metal spike on less formal occasions. Officers' star badges were enamelled in the centre.

The superveste was also re-introduced in 1843 having been held in abeyance since the time of Frederick the Great. This red superveste was edged in white, pleated at the lower end and piped all round in red. On the chest and back was a white embroidered star of the order of the black eagle. For officers the star was embroidered in silver and edges of the superveste were in silver lace. The tunic worn underneath was white, single-breasted, and fastened with hooks and eyes. On each side of the opening edge was a row of white lace, edged in red. The coat was piped red on the sleeve seams and around the shoulder straps. The skirt was cut full at this period, similar to the civilian fashion. The back slashes were piped red and ornamented with three buttons of white metal. The standing collar was red, edged silver, with a silver lace bar each side. White breeches were worn, with tall black leather boots. The pouch belt was white and the leather pouch black, with the star badge of the order of the black eagle in white metal. Officers' pouch belts were of silver lace and their pouches were embroidered in silver. The style of this uniform was introduced by the Russians and copied by King Frederick William IV of Prussia.

On mounted occasions a brass cuirass was worn, edged in white metal and ornamented with brass studs. Brass scales over the shoulders fastened the cuirass. On gala occasions the Garde du Corps wore black cuirasses which had been presented by the Tsar of Russia. Officers wore a sash of silver with two black lines running through and continued into the silver fringe tassels. The heavy cavalry sword had a steel scabbard with a brass half-basket hilt. The sword knot was silver and black for all ranks. Officers in court dress wore the same helmet, but with a scarlet tunic piped blue with a standing collar of blue edged in silver lace. Silver epaulettes with silver fringes were worn. The rounded cuffs were blue and ornamented with two bars of silver lace and silver buttons. The sash was the same and also the silver pouch belt. White gloves were worn in place of the gauntlets. On ballroom occasions at the court, officers dispensed with the sword, sash and pouch belt.

[PLATE 57

Rome 1970

THE NOBLE GUARD

The Noble Guard of His Holiness was founded in 1801, to replace the Papal cavalry disbanded in 1798 on the constitution of the Republic. The ranks of the Noble Guard are drawn from aristocratic families – whose title must be at least one hundred years old – and from the provinces of the Papal State. The commandant has the rank of lieutenant general. The commandant is the standard-bearer for the Holy Roman Church and the Noble Guard has the great honour of direct personal protection of the sacred person of His Holiness. On each day an officer and six guards are on duty at the throne room and the secret antechamber.

The Guard has never fought in action. When the Pope went into exile during the Napoleonic Wars men of the Guard were imprisoned in Castel Sant'Angelo until re-established in 1814.

The helmet is the Italian dragoon pattern, brass with a black metal turban. An eight-pointed gilt star bears the papal arms. The brass crest has the form of a lion's head and from this rises a black hair plume. From the left side issues a white standing plume.

The double-breasted tunic is of scarlet cloth with two rows of gilt brass buttons. The collar is embroidered in gold wire. The epaulettes are gold with gold straps and bullion fringes, the tops ornamented with stars to denote the rank of the wearer. The blue standing collar is laced all round in gold with only a centre light of blue showing between the gold lace. The pouch belt is of crimson leather edged in gold lace and gold stripes across, and the waist belt is of gold lace with a red line at the top and bottom. The circular gilt brass buckle has the same design as the helmet plate. The white leather breeches fit into tall jackboots of black leather. The sword belt is of gold lace on crimson leather. The sword has a white metal hilt and scabbard with a gold lace sword knot and tassel. White gauntlet gloves are worn on parade.

On less formal occasions a blue tunic is worn, single-breasted with a standing collar, laced as the gala dress tunic. The epaulettes and belt are also the same. The helmet is worn without the black falling plume or the egret side plume.

The entrances to the Vatican and Vatican City are in the custody of the Swiss Guard, who also guard the Pope's summer residence at Castel Gandolfo. There is also the Palatine Guard, formed in 1850, and drawn from the citizens of Rome. The pontifical gendarmerie in gala dress wear a bearskin cap with red plumes. The black coatees have a standing collar laced in silver, and silver epaulettes with silver fringes. The sleeve is decorated with an austrian knot in silver russia braid. From the left shoulder is fitted a silver cord epaulette. The sword hangs from a cross-belt worn over the right shoulder. The sword knot is silver with a silver tassel. White breeches and black leather jackboots as well as white gauntlet gloves are worn.

57 Rome – The Noble Guard 1970

58 Rumania – Royal Escort 1927

PLATE 58]

Rumania 1927

ROYAL ESCORT

King Carol of Rumania had a personal escort dressed in the Prussian style. The helmet, similar to that of the Imperial German cuirassiers, was of white metal with brass fittings. The helmet plate was the cypher of King Carol with a crown above; a cockade on each side of the chin scale terminal also followed the Prussian pattern, in the Rumanian national colours; red, yellow and blue. The horse-hair plume was white and could be replaced by a spike when on other duties. The tunic was of pearl grey cloth with four patch pockets. The standing collar was of dark blue, as also were the shoulder straps. The coat was fastened by six brass buttons and piped in dark blue. From the right shoulder hung a yellow aiguillette with brass points. The waist belt was white as also were the gauntlet gloves.

The breeches were of dark blue cloth and fitted into tall black jackboots. The spurs were of white metal. The officer's uniform was similar in most details; the helmet had gilt fittings, the tunic had pleated pockets and the shoulder straps were piped in gold cord. Officers wore a gold lace pouch belt mounted on scarlet morocco leather. Their aiguillette was made of gold cord with gilt metal ends. The waist belt, also Prussian in style, was gold with a woven line of red, yellow and blue, the national colours. On mounted duties the shabraque was of dark blue cloth, edged with two rows of gold lace. The corners were embroidered in gold with the Royal cypher and crown, as were the pistol holsters.

In 1931 King Carol introduced the tunic that had been regulation before the First World War. This was of dark blue cloth with a standing collar of black, laced all round in gold. The front of the tunic was piped in black and fastened by six gilt brass buttons. The epaulettes were of gold lace with a centre black line. The fringes were gold bullion, and on the right shoulder hung a gold and black aiguillette. The gold lace pouch belt was lined with scarlet morocco leather as worn with the earlier uniform. The turnbacks of the tunic were scarlet. The waist-belt was that worn on the 1924 uniform.

The sword had a gilt half-basket hilt of four bars. The scabbard was of black metal suspended by one ring. The sword sling was of brown leather and fastened under the tunic with a web belt. In the late 1930s a metal cuirass is thought to have been worn by the Mounted Royal Escort.

Harness was brown leather with brass fittings except the bit and stirrups which were of white metal. The white throat plume was suspended from a brown leather fitting.

Rumanian history is confusing because of the abdication and return of King Carol. In 1927 King Ferdinand died and was succeeded by his grandson King Michael. Carol had renounced his titles in 1925 and gone into exile. In 1930 he returned and was proclaimed King and his son, Michael, Crown Prince. In 1940, King Carol again abdicated under pressure from Germany.

[PLATE 59

Russia 1830

PAVLOWSKY GRENADIER GUARDS

The Russian guard regiments were distinguished by names rather than numbers. The guard included regiments such as Moscovski, Iegerski, Ismailovski, Semenovski, Preobzhenski, Pavlovski, Lithvania, Finland: Kegsholm Volinski and Petersburg. The Russian Imperial Guard had been formed by Peter the Great, Tsar of Russia, after observing the armies of other European States. All the guard regiments were commanded by generals and the battalions by colonels.

It is an interesting note that the tall mitre caps worn by the Pavlowski Grenadier Guards were the same as those worn at the Battle of Friedland in 1807. This guard regiment entered the Guards Brigade on 13 April 1813. The Russian army at this time was some eight thousand men strong and had reached the pinnacle of achievement, at least as far as the military tailors were concerned.

The grenadier cap introduced in 1825 had a brass front depicting the double-headed eagle of Russia with a shield on the breast engraved with St George and the Dragon. The body was of white cloth with a red top and white piping. The chin strap was of brass scales from brass grenades at each side of the cap. The tuft at the peak of the head-dress was white wool for the grenadiers and in silver wire for officers. Upon entry to the Brigade of Guards the regiment adopted the dark green coatee, with standing collar piped in red. The collar had two bars of gold lace for officers and for the grenadiers it was in white. The coatee had a red plastron front with two rows of brass buttons on the outer edges. Officers' coatees were adorned with bullion epaulettes, with a fringe for officers of field rank. For the men the shoulder straps were plain red. The rounded cuffs were of red cloth, with a red slash ornamented with three bars of lace to match the collar. The coatee tails had red turnbacks. Officers on duty wore a gorget; for field officers of gilt brass and for junior officers of silver. Around the waist, officers wore a silver sash with silver fringes hanging on the left side. From a frog fitting on the left hip a sword with a brass hilt was suspended in a scabbard of leather with gilt fittings. The sword knot was silver. White trousers were worn in summer; for the grenadiers these were in the form of gaiters that buttoned up the side as far as the knee. The equipment was of white leather, the pack covered with fur. The muskets had a red rifle sling.

In winter green trousers were worn. These were piped along the outer seam with red and the plastron front could be worn buttoned over the red piping. Officers' greatcoats were of green cloth with a standing collar piped red, and double-breasted front piped in the same way, as were cuffs and back slashes. A cocked hat with a green feather was worn for walking out.

59 Russia – Pavlowsky Grenadier Guards 1830

60 Russia – Cuirassier Empress Chevalier Guards 1862

PLATE 60]

Russian 1862

CUIRASSIER EMPRESS CHEVALIER GUARDS

Members of this regiment wore a brass helmet, on top of which was the Russian double-headed eagle in white metal. The chin-scales were made of brass and scarlet lined. The badge plate was the Star of the Order of St Andrew.

A single-breasted coatee of white cloth was fastened with brass buttons and the shoulder straps were of red cloth, piped in white. The high collar was also of red cloth, but embroidered with gold lace. Brass or brassed metal, bound in white metal, was used to make the cuirass front and back plates, which had scaled fasteners bound with red leather. These were lined in red cloth to keep the metal from rubbing the coatee. The belt fastener was of red leather. The cuirass itself was lined on the inside in white leather.

On dismounted duties the guardsmen carried muskets and the cuirass was not worn. In its place was a superveste shaped like the cuirass, made of red cloth edged with blue, and bound with gold lace. Around the waist and fitted to the superveste was a scalloped blue cloth edged with gold lace.

The star badge on the chest was also the Order of St Andrew, as on the helmet. A cross-belt and gauntlet gloves of white leather were worn. Napoleon type high knee-boots, made of lacquered leather, were worn over trousers of white material. The sword had a three-bar hilt in brass and the grip was made of fish-skin bound in silver wire. The sword was carried in a steel scabbard.

[PLATE 61

Sardinia 1848

GRENADIER GUARDS

The Kingdom of Sardinia was to cause constant confusion because the King of Sardinia was also ruler of Piedmont, Duke of Savoy and Count of Nice. These various countries were only connected by the personal ties of the king. At this period the King was Charles Albert, whose son unified Italy and the House of Savoy under one ruler.

In the war with Austria, the Sardinian army was completely defeated by Marshal Radetsky at the Battle of Novara. Charles Albert was forced to abdicate and retired, to die in a monastery. Rome was occupied by a French army to protect the Pope and the Papal States. Unification of Italy was not complete until the withdrawal after the Franco-Prussian War in September 1870, when after slight resistance the Italian army was able to breach the walls and enter the Holy City.

The uniform of the guards followed closely the fashion of France as did the rest of the Sardinian army. The bearskin caps were fitted with large brass grenade badges. Around the body of the cap passed red cords ending in red tassels on the right side, which led down to a further set of tassels and cords fastened to the jacket. The top of the bearskin had a red cloth inset with a white cross placed upon it. The coat was of blue cloth, double-breasted with two rows of white metal buttons. The standing collar was red, ornamented with a bar of white lace. The blue cloth shoulder straps were piped red and ended with red wool tufts at the sleeves. Around the waist was worn a white leather belt with a brass buckle engraved with a grenade badge. This belt supported the bayonet frog and a short sword, both worn on the same fitting. The sword had a brass hilt and a black leather scabbard with brass fittings. The black glazed leather pack was held by two white leather straps that passed over the shoulders and fitted to the waist belt. On the right side of the waist belt was worn a black leather ammunition pouch decorated with a brass grenade. The trousers were of blue cloth with a red piping down the outer seam. Black spats were worn over the black leather boots.

The officer's uniform differed in having silver cords and tassels encircling the bearskin. The standing collar was ornamented with a bar of silver lace. The shoulders carried a pair of silver epaulettes with silver bullions. The round cuffs were decorated with a bar of lace, as was the collar. The officer's sword belt was of white leather with white straps and was worn over a sky-blue sash, the tassels hanging on the left side. The sword had a gilt brass hilt with a gold sword knot and tassel. The black leather scabbard had brass fittings. The officer's trousers had a broad red stripe down the outer seam. Officers usually wore short white gloves, even on campaign.

61 Sardinia – Grenadier Guards 1848

62 Saxe Gotha – Garde du Corps 1758

PLATE 62]

Saxe-Gotha 1758

GARDE DU CORPS

This small state ruled by the Duke of Saxe-Gotha had a very small army indeed, but of course the formation of a Garde du Corps for the ceremonial rather than practical guard for the Palace was considered most necessary. This regiment consisted of a troop of seventy-five men who were housed in the ducal palace at Gotha.

The hat at this time was the black felt tricorne, bound around the edge with silver lace, on the left side a loop of silver russia braid and a silver button securing a black and silver bow. The hat was held to the head by a black tape which passed under the queue at the back of the neck.

The coat was of yellow cloth. The buff cavalry coat had now finally disappeared. The fall-down collar was red, and edged in two rows of silver lace with a pattern of lace between. The shoulder straps were plain red, edged in silver cord. The coat was fastened at the waist with hooks and eyes, the leading edges laced in a similar manner to the collar. It was now the fashion to fasten the coats back when marching or riding, usually by means of a button or hook at the bottom edge of the coat. The coat turnbacks repeated the lace pattern and revealed a yellow silk lining. The deep turnback cuffs were red and edged in silver lace to match the collar. The half-gauntlet gloves partly hid the cuffs and were made of yellow or buff leather. The red silk sash passed tightly around the waist and was fastened at the front. On the left hip hung a sabretache, supported by three white leather straps with gilt fastenings. The sabretache was of red cloth edged in silver lace to match the coat. On the face was embroidered in gold and silver wire the crest of Saxe-Gotha.

The heavy cavalry sword had a half-basket brass hilt with the Royal arms on the guard. The straight steel blade fitted into a brass scabbard with insets of black leather. The sword knot was of silver lace with a gold bullion tassel. The buff breeches fitted into black leather jackboots with steel spurs. Officers on foot affected a walking cane.

The Court at Gotha at this time was remarkable for its taste for literature and sciences. The Crown Prince was a mathematician of some note, the Duchess was in correspondence with Voltaire, and the Duke's younger son was a patron of literature. French was the language spoken at Court, and it was at this time that the *Almanach de Gotha* was first published, the original 'Who's Who' for the nobility of Europe.

[PLATE 63

Saxony 1811

GARDE DU CORPS

The tall brass helmet had a ponyskin turban, and placed around the turban was a gilt laurel wreath. A brass ridge at the top of the helmet supported a bearskin crest. From the left side issued a white plume. The chin scales were of gilt brass. The coatee, piped light blue, was canary yellow, fastened with hooks and eyes and laced down the centre in gold. The collar was light blue laced in gold at the front and lower edge. The epaulettes were gold lace with heavy gold bullions. The turnbacks to the coatee were pale blue. From the right shoulder was hung a gold cord aiguillette fastened to the tunic under a cross-belt. This pouch belt was of gold lace on a pale blue leather backing and was ornamented with silver chains and pickers. The waist belt, similar to the pouch belt, was of gold lace on pale blue leather. The gilt buckle had a silver monogram crest. Short white gauntlet gloves were worn in review order. Buff breeches were worn with tall jackboots. The sword had a straight blade and a basket hilt of gilt metal. The black leather scabbard had gilt brass mountings and the sword knot was silver.

The pale blue shabraque was edged in gold lace, and the pistol housings and lower edge of the shabraque were embroidered with the King of Saxony's monogram, *Frederick I.*

Frederick had unfortunately sided with the French during the Napoleonic Wars and had again disastrously sided with Napoleon after Leipzig.

Besides the Garde du Corps there was also one regiment of cuirassiers of the guard, wearing a yellow coatee as the Garde du Corps – but this was altered in 1810 to white with red facings, a black cuirass lined in red, and buff breeches with black leather jackboots. The helmet was similar to that of the Garde du Corps. This cuirassier regiment was promoted to Guard status after its brave conduct at the Battle of Friedland in 1807, but could trace its history back to 1660. The black cuirass consisted of only the front plate, a feature of the Saxon service. This regiment existed up to the end of the First World War.

The infantry grenadiers of the guard wore a bearskin cap with white twisted cords and tassels hanging on the right-hand side and a brass plate at the front displaying the arms of the Kingdom of Saxony. The coatee was scarlet with a standing collar of yellow, the plastron front buttoned back to reveal yellow facings which were fastened by six white metal buttons. The turnbacks were also yellow. On the shoulders were worn epaulettes with white straps and white wool fringes, and over the left shoulder passed a buff leather belt to support the black leather ammunition pouch, which displayed the arms of Saxony in brass. The cuffs were rounded, yellow. White breeches fitted into white gaiters that buttoned up the sides with brass buttons. The sword worn on the left side had a brass stirrup hilt.

63 Saxony – Garde du Corps 1811

64 Scotland – Bodyguard for Scotland 1911

PLATE 64]

Scotland 1911

BODYGUARD FOR SCOTLAND

The Sovereign's Bodyguard for Scotland was formed in 1676 by Scottish noblemen, to encourage archery. When George IV visited Scotland in 1822 he confirmed them in the title of Bodyguards. The Earl of Hopetoun became the first captain general of the King's Bodyguard for Scotland, the Royal Company of Archers. This bodyguard travelled to India in 1911 for the Coronation Durbar of King George V at Delhi.

At Court the head-dress is a black cocked hat with a gold loop and gold tassels at the ends. The plume is of green cock-tail feathers. The green cloth coatee is double-breasted with two rows of nine gilt buttons. The standing collar is of green velvet and embroidered in gold wire. The slashed cuffs are embroidered in gold wire and have three gilt buttons on each slash. The skirts, edged with green, form the turnbacks and have a gold embroidered thistle at the bottom of each skirt and two gilt buttons at the back to support the sash. The coatee is lined in green silk. The gold epaulettes have straps of green velvet embroidered in gold wire and gold bullion fringes. Around the waist is worn a crimson silk sash with two tassels hanging on the left hip, behind the sword.

The sword, carried in a green velvet frog, has gilt mountings with a silver grip. The scabbard is in black leather with gilt and chased mountings. The trousers are green cloth with a stripe of $1\frac{3}{4}$ inch gold lace along the outer seams. Strips of patent leather button under the black boots. Officers wear an aiguillette on the right shoulder and have a gold sash with three stripes of crimson, the tassels gold and crimson. On less formal occasions officers wear this uniform with the Kilmarnock bonnet and twisted gold cord shoulder straps.

The field uniform consists of a bonnet of the Kilmarnock type with a crimson tourie, a green and white cockade and eagle feathers, the number depending on the rank of the wearer. A frosted gilt badge is worn on the front of the bonnet. The dark green coat has a standing collar edged in black braid. The coat is edged all round with a black mohair braid with a red light on the inner edge. The coat has four panels of frogging across the chest also piped red, and the gauntlet cuffs are treated in a similar manner. The epaulettes are of twisted cord. The black leather waist belt supports the sword on the left hip. Across the breast, over the left shoulder, is worn a baldrick of green cloth edged in black mohair braid with red piping. The trousers are green with black mohair braid stripes piped red, and white gloves are worn except when using the bow.

[PLATE 65

Senegal 1970

PRESIDENTIAL GUARD GENDARMERIE

The French used Senegal troops in the First World War and they were regarded as very good quality soldiers. French traders and explorers had been resident in Senegal since the seventeenth century. The French were, however, driven out in 1720, but the Seven Years War returned the country to them, and other parts were re-captured during the American War of Independence. In 1783 the Treaty of Paris confirmed the French in these possessions. Because of various revolutions at home, France had to abandon this colony until 1852, when there was a campaign to clear the country of slave traders and a new French administration was adopted. By the turn of the century Senegal troops were being trained into a force of three battalions of infantry and a squadron of Spahis. Small parties were placed in the villages, commanded by a lieutenant or sub-lieutenant.

In the First World War there were thirty-seven battalions, ten batteries and two companies of engineers, a total of about 215,000 soldiers.

This Presidential Guard wears a uniform which has characteristics carried on from the days of French colonisation and dating back to the latter half of the nineteenth century when native troops were recruited by the French. The red felt tarbush has a white line around the centre, and carries at the front a brass cap badge in the form of a grenade and star. The head-dress is held on by a red leather chin-strap.

The shell jacket is of red cloth with rounded cuffs without facings and is fastened by means of six brass buttons. From the left shoulder hangs a blue twisted aiguillette with brass points. The loose breeches are light blue in colour and are ornamented on the outer seam with a white lace austrian knot pattern from the waist down to the boots, which are of black leather fitted with white metal spurs. Over the shoulders a red cloak is worn. A brown leather harness strap over the right shoulder supports a bandolier of leather ammunition pouches around the waist. From a strap on the left hip hangs the sword, of the French light cavalry pattern with brass hilt, in an all-steel scabbard. The sword knot is of red leather.

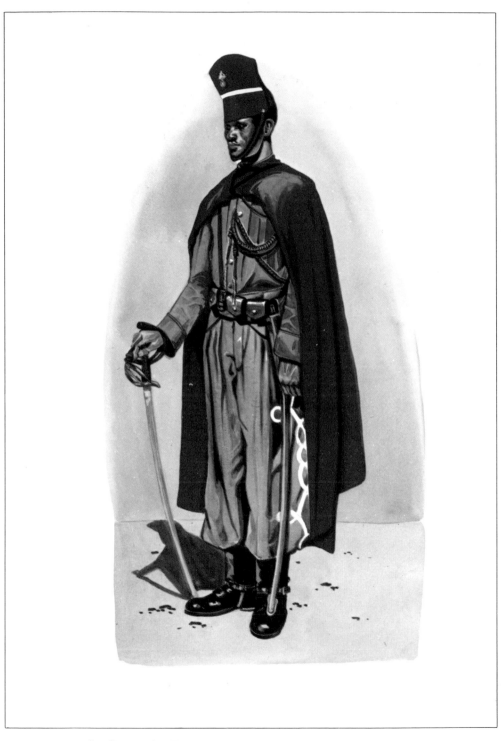

65 Senegal – Presidential Guard Gendarmerie 1970

66 Sikkim – Royal Bodyguard 1970

PLATE 66]

Sikkim 1970

ROYAL BODYGUARD

The small Kingdom of Sikkim lies between Nepal and Bhutan on the northern borders of India. The king had a personal guard of sixty men, drawn from the forest-dwelling Lepchas, Sikkim's original inhabitants. It is a tradition that the Rajah of Sikkim came from Eastern Tibet. The State was invaded twice by the Gurkhas in the eighteenth century. At the outbreak of the Nepal War in 1815 between the British and the Nepalese there was formed an alliance between Sikkim and the British, and afterwards some territory was ceded to them. In 1835 a punitive expedition was sent into Sikkim because of the imprisonment of British officials by the Rajah and he had to cede the site of the present town of Darjeeling and pay an indemnity for fifteen years. Sikkim became a peaceful State under the British Raj. In 1947 Sikkim entered an interim agreement with India, similar to that previously agreed with the British.

The head-dress is made of cane. In all Sikkim only one old Lepcha still weaves them. The cap badge is silver, a crescent moon clasping the royal arms. From a red woven receptacle stands a plume of peacock and king crow feathers. The hat is held on by a white cord under the chin. The coat is of red cloth decorated with black designs. The black pointed cuffs have a small austrian knot. The front of the coat is fastened with four rows of silver frogging. A white neckerchief is tucked into the top of the coat. The white breeches have an overgarment of white with gold and black lace stripes. Blue woven stockings with a red flash on the garter fit into black laced boots.

The armament consists of a muzzle-loading flintlock gun, part of a gift from Queen Victoria, as Empress of India. Around the waist is occasionally worn a brown leather belt with a white metal clasp ornamented with the royal coat of arms.

The musicians of the Guard wear a coat of red cloth decorated all round with a strip of leopard-skin fur. The coat is piped in black cord, within the leopard skin.

[PLATE 67

South Africa 1969

PRESIDENTIAL GUARD

This guard serves as a Guard of Honour for the President of South Africa at Pretoria. The uniform reflects the earlier Republic of South Africa, the Orange Free State.

The shako is a blue felt bound in gold, similar in shape to the Swiss army head-dress of the late nineteenth century. The badge at the front depicts the arms of South Africa on a shield. The plume is a black ostrich feather. The tunic has four rows of frogging in an orange-gold colour. The tunic itself is in grey-green. The sleeves have an austrian knot design. The collar has a metal badge of brass with two letters S.P. The shoulder straps are piped in orange-gold cord; the base has a decoration of four rows of cord in the same colour. Four brass buttons fasten the tunic at the centre of the frogging. The trousers are grey-green with a row of orange-gold lace along the outer seam. White gloves and a leather belt with a brass buckle complete the uniform. Officers wear a similar uniform except that the waist belt is of gold lace; with it they wear a dagger similar to that worn by French officers.

This unit is an active part of the regular army and is trained in the same manner.

Previous to the formation of the South African Republic there was no particular guard unit, although there were several elite volunteer regiments which had acted as guards on the various occasions when one was required. These included the Cape Peninsular Rifles, the Cape Town Highlanders and a cavalry regiment called Prince Alfred's Own Cape Town Cavalry, which existed until 1889. They wore a metal helmet with gilt fittings, the dragon pattern used in the British cavalry. The fittings were gilt and the falling plume, white. The shell jacket was light blue with a standing collar. Eight silver buttons fastened the jacket, which was single-breasted. The collar and cuffs were white and laced in silver. The pouch belt was silver with a centre stripe of blue, the whole mounted on sky-blue leather. The lancer girdle was gold with two red stripes, the sabretache blue with a silver binding, and embroidered in the centre was the crown monogram CTC and an ornamental leaf design. The shabraque was the same with a broad silver lace edge.

The Boer Republic also had units dressed for gala occasions. The Transvaal Artillery and the Orange Free State Artillery were perhaps the most famous, with blue uniforms ornamented with gold austrian knots following the style then popular in Holland and France. There were also many volunteer regiments.

67 South Africa – Presidential Guard 1969

68 Spain – Albarderos 1896

PLATE 68]

Spain 1896

ALBARDEROS

The closest guard to the King of Spain's person was formed by the Albarderos. The uniform dated from the eighteenth century and remained unchanged until 1931 when the guard was disbanded on the departure of Alphonso XIII. The force was drawn from the aristocratic families of Spain. The name is taken from the halberd, the weapon carried on ceremonial duties in and about the palaces. The Albarderos consisted of forty officers and two hundred and fifty men. They were ranked quite differently from the rest of the army. A colonel would be appointed captain and a lieutenant a first lieutenant and so on, until a first lieutenant would be appointed corporal. All officers of the regular army were eligible for the Guard.

The head-dress consisted of a black felt bicorne hat, laced all round in silver, on the right side a cockade in the national colours of red, gold and red, held by a silver cord and button. The blue cloth coatee was cut in the style of the eighteenth century, but with a standing collar of red cloth edged in silver lace. The plastron front was cut away to the waist, but fastened from neck to mid-chest with hooks and eyes. The plastron was red and edged in silver lace, with six silver buttons on the lower part and one at the top of the plastron. The white waistcoat was edged in silver lace and fastened with silver buttons. The two small pockets were also edged in silver lace. The round gauntlet cuffs were red, edged with silver lace on the upper part. The buff breeches fitted into black gaiters that buttoned up the side with cloth buttons. The shoes were black.

At the waist was carried a court sword with gilt hilt and red sword knot and tassel. The halberd had a cross-formed blade of steel; the ornamental tassel at the head was of red silk.

The undress uniform was a plain blue single-breasted tail coat fastened by a single row of silver buttons. The trousers were dark blue. A cloak of white cloth with a stand-and-fall collar of red cloth and a lining of red silk was also worn.

The Albarderos were not mounted and did not accompany the king outside the palace, except on special occasions when the king walked on foot, such as the ceremony to honour those that died in the Madrid Uprising 2 May 1808.

In the mid-nineteenth century silver epaulettes were adopted and the plastron worn fastened at the waist; the sword was carried by a belt over the right shoulder. Later, however, there was a return to the more traditional uniform of the eighteenth century.

[PLATE 69

Sudan 1969

PRESIDENTIAL GUARD

A mounted troop as well as foot troops form the Sudanese Presidential Guard. Sudan was administered by the British and Egyptians, and it was hoped, by the Egyptians, that the Sudanese would choose to be part of a Great Egypt; however, this was not to be. The Egyptian government had declared Farouk King of Egypt and the Sudan, but the British would not recognise this and plans proceeded for Sudanese self-government. The Presidential Guard of Sudan is based at Khartoum and mounts guard at the Old Governor's Palace, now the Presidential Residence, which stands on the bank of the Nile. The original palace was destroyed during the Mahdi Uprising in 1885 when the city was captured and General Gordon, Governor General of the Sudan, was killed. The city was ruined, and not until 1898 was Khartoum recaptured by Anglo-Egyptians under Kitchener. The palace was subsequently restored and Khartoum became the capital of Sudan.

The white turban of the head-dress has the ends fringed and tucked into the upper fold to form a fan effect. This fringe is in the Sudanese colours of blue, yellow and green. A woven piece of the turban in these colours is visible passing over the crown. The jacket is olive green drab, single-breasted, with five white metal buttons fastening down the front, and two patch pockets on the breast, also with white metal buttons. The stand-up collar is plain. The shoulder straps are edged in gold cord and the ends have a gold fringe falling over the shoulders. An aiguillette of yellow cords is worn over the right shoulder. The sleeves have two white metal buttons. Around the waist is worn a white leather belt to carry the bayonet frog with a simple brass buckle. The trousers are of the same material as the tunic, with yellow piping down the outer seam. White gaiters are worn over black boots. The rifles carry a white sling. White gloves are worn on ceremonial duties.

69 Sudan – Presidential Guard 1969

70 Sweden – Life Guards 1807

PLATE 70]

Sweden 1807

LIFE GUARDS

The Life Guard of Gustavus Adolphus IV consisted of two regiments. The officers' cocked hats were of black felt, edged with two rows of silver lace, and to one side a yellow bow with silver russia cord and a button supported a white feather plume. The coatee was of blue cloth, faced in yellow for the 1st regiment and red for the 2nd. The collar was ornamented with two rows of silver lace and embroidery. The plastron front was laced in a similar fashion. Rounded cuffs carried the same embroidery and lace. The lining of the coat tails was in the facing colour. The open front of the coatee revealed a white waistcoat which was fastened with silver buttons. Over all this passed a white leather sword belt which fastened with an oblong buckle of silver, bearing the Swedish arms in gilt. The epaulettes were of silver lace with silver bullions. White breeches fitted into the short black boots and were ornamented with silver lace. The sword had a gilt hilt with a black leather scabbard with gilt fittings. The sword knot was of gold lace with a gold tassel.

The 2nd regiment was dressed in the same manner, except that the collar was yellow and the plastron, cuffs and turnbacks were red. The guardsmen wore a head-dress peculiar to this country. It was of leather, the brim being drawn up on the left-hand side with a silver button and plume. A black crest was fitted to the top of the hat. On a brass band on the front was the crest of Vasa with a crown above. The guardsmen differed in the wearing of a plain white lace, and wore breeches and gaiters. Over the left shoulder was a white leather belt with a black leather ammunition pouch ornamented with a brass badge depicting the three crowns of Sweden within a shield, with a crown over all.

In 1809 the king was forced to abdicate, having lost Finland to Russia. He eventually died insane after settling in Switzerland. After the death of two very elderly princes, Sweden chose Marshal Bernadotte, related by marriage to Napoleon.

The Life Guards included one squadron dressed and equipped as Mounted Rifles. They wore a black leather helmet ornamented with a white falling hair plume, and a white standing feather plume. A silver star encompassed at the front the arms of Vasa. The coatee was of green cloth with a plastron front piped in white, with bars of white lace across in pairs. The coat fastened down the centre with white metal buttons. The standing collar was green, piped white. The shoulder cords were white and fastened with a white metal button. The cuffs were pointed and edged white. Gauntlet gloves were worn over them. White breeches fitted into black leather boots with 'V' tops. A black leather waist belt carried the ammunition pouch at the front for easy access. This was decorated with a white metal crest of the Vasa. Two black leather cross-belts supported the carbine on the right, and on the left the curved light cavalry sword with a steel hilt. The scabbard was of black leather with steel mountings.

[PLATE 71

Thailand 1970

ROYAL PALACE GUARD

The Royal Palace Guard of Thailand wears a uniform which is a mixture of East and West. The cap of black velvet is completely Eastern in character. It is laced around the body and on the quarters. It also has earflaps which are gold laced on the outer edge. On the top is a gilt pagoda-like ornament. At the front is a gilt badge of the garunda bird, the crest of the kings of Thailand.

The tunic is European in style, being made of ultramarine cloth, single-breasted and edged with broad gold lace. On the shoulders are twisted gold cord epaulettes. The collar is gold laced and bears on each side in silver the Royal cypher. The collar and cuffs are rose pink. The cuffs, embroidered with stars to denote the rank, are gauntlet-shape and gold laced all round. The waist is encircled by a sash of gold with a dark rose red centre, the tassels and fringes, mixed dark rose red and gold, hang on the left side. What appears to be knee breeches is in fact a loincloth called a panury, made of silk. This garment is usually about two feet wide and about seven feet long. The ends are passed between the legs and this gives the impression from the front of knee breeches. The panury is heavily ornamented with gold lace on the lower edge. White silk stockings and black shoes complete the outfit. The sword, of traditional Thai design, is carried from a gold laced baldrick over the right shoulder, passing under the epaulette.

The Thailand sovereign is also served by a Royal Foot Guard Regiment. This is dressed in a European manner, influenced by British or British-Indian military fashions. The white pith helmet has a brass chin scale, and the helmet badge in gilt depicts the crest of Thailand. The plume is of black hair. The coat is of scarlet cloth with a standing collar, dark blue with gold piping. It is embroidered in gold wire with a leaf design. The blue cloth shoulder straps are embroidered around the edge in gold. The coat is single-breasted and fastened by seven silver buttons. The pointed cuffs are dark blue and embroidered in gold. The silver lace waist sash has two lines of scarlet running through which continue into the tassels that hang on the left-hand side. The trousers are dark blue with a red stripe each side of the piping. From the right shoulder is fastened a gold aiguillette hooked to the second button. The sword has a white metal hilt and scabbard and a gold sword knot.

On other than formal duties the guard is dressed in Western combat uniform based on the American pattern.

71 Thailand – Royal Palace Guard 1970

72 Tunisia – Spahis of the Guard 1970

PLATE 72]

Tunisia 1970

SPAHIS OF THE GUARD

The President of Tunisia's bodyguard, called Spahis, derive their name from the Turkish cavalry of that name. The French gave the same title to the light cavalry formed in the North African colonies, of which Tunisia was once part until the Independence in 1957.

The white turban head-dress has bands of red holding the brass cap badge depicting the arms of Tunisia. The burnous or cloak is white, lined in red, with a red hood drawn over the back. This hood is edged in white. The shell jacket is worn open without fasteners, and is edged with white, with pointed cuffs also edged in white. The shirt worn under the jacket is red. This also has a white front to the fastening edge. Around the waist is worn a red cummerbund over which is fastened, by a white metal buckle, the white leather sword belt. The sword is a French pattern with a single ring fastening to the metal scabbard. The hilt is of brass.

The loose fitting trousers, characteristic of North African desert cavalry, have a design down each outer side in white. The brown leather boots, with brown leather gaiters, are fitted with white metal spurs. The national colours of Tunisia are red and white, hence the predominant use of these colours for the Presidential Guard.

The main difference between the previous French uniform is the use of red trousers in place of the blue ones which were common to most of the French North African mounted troops of Spahis.

The French extended their North African Empire in 1881 by declaring a Protectorate over Tunisia. This action brought about a break in diplomatic relations between France and Italy, who had designs on that territory herself. The conquest was enforced by twelve thousand men, under the command of General Forgemol de Bostquenard, who were transported from Toulouse. After several small battles at El Kef, Tabarka and the fortress at Sfax, which was reduced by the French navy, a treaty was signed at Bardo, the Palace of the Bey of Tunis, the ruler of the country. He had first declared his independence from Turkey in 1871, and now ten years later was under the Protection of France. By 1882 the pacification of the country was complete. The French were soon recruiting for native regiments on the style of those raised in Algeria. These regiments subsequently fought in Morocco and later in the First World War, and numbered some fifty thousand troops.

On Independence in 1957, the Bey abdicated and a republic was instituted. One of the Tunisian Spahis cavalry regiments was subsequently promoted to the title of 'The Spahis of the Presidential Guard'.

[PLATE 73

Turkey 1854

INTERIOR GUARD, BEYLERBEY PALACE

At the time of the Crimean War the Turkish army was assuming a more Western approach to uniforms and military technology, and adopted more or less the French fashion. It employed French military advisors from about 1820. In the uniform of the various palace guards, however, the sultan was rather conservative, and a mixture of Eastern and Western styles prevailed. The Guard of the 'Prince-of-Princes' Palace wore a uniform of this sort.

The head-dress was a tall cap of pleated red cloth on a bamboo frame bound at the bottom with gold lace. The chin strap was of gilt brass scales lined in red morocco leather. The front of the cap was decorated with a scalloped design in gilt, above which, from a gilt holder, sprang a white hair plume. From behind the crown of the cap hung a fringed gold cloth. The coat was of red cloth, single-breasted and fastened by nine gilt buttons, enclosed in nine scallop-edged gold lace bars, each of these terminating in another gilt button. This pattern was repeated on the other side of the jacket front. The standing collar was piped in gold lace and filled with gold lace to the full depth of the collar, so that no cloth showed. The pointed cuffs were edged in a gold lace and the whole space between the lace and the edge of the cuff embroidered in gold wire. Round the waist was worn a gold lace belt on red morocco leather, supporting the sword. The lower part of the coat, which reached the knees, was edged in broad gold lace, the leading points embroidered with a scalloped pattern in gold wire. The trousers were of green cloth, tight fitting, and fastened under the shoe with a button. The outer seam was covered by a broad gold lace stripe. The boots were black.

The guardsmen were armed with an ivory-hilted scimitar in a black leather sheath with gilt brass fittings. There was no sword knot. The main arm of the guardsman was a halberd with a black staff, quite plain and without decoration.

The regular army at this time had French style uniforms; single-breasted tunics of blue cloth with a standing collar and slashed cuffs, and trousers of blue cloth with a red stripe down the outer seam. A red fez was worn by all ranks.

The cavalry wore a blue tunic with hussar frogging ornamented by three rows of brass buttons, and blue overalls with red stripes. Their armament consisted of lances and cavalry sabres.

73 Turkey – Interior Guard Beylerbey Palace 1854

74 United Kingdom – The Honourable Corps of Gentlemen at Arms 1970

PLATE 74]

United Kingdom 1970

THE HONOURABLE CORPS OF GENTLEMEN AT ARMS

The nearest Guard to the Sovereign of the United Kingdom is the Honourable Corps of Gentlemen at Arms. This Corps was raised by King Henry VIII and first employed in 1513 during the French campaign.

The helmet, in use since 1848, is of white metal with gilt mountings and chin scales with lions' heads bosses. The 18-inch-long falling plume is of white swan feathers. The badge depicts the royal coat of arms with the crown above on a cut silver star. The coatee is of scarlet cloth in a pattern adopted in 1838. It is single-breasted and fastened by nine gilt brass buttons down the front. These display the garter star and garter with tudor portcullis in the centre. The standing collar is of royal blue velvet embroidered in solid gold wire with a silver portcullis each side. The cuffs are of royal blue velvet and are embroidered in a similar manner but without the portcullis. The epaulettes are boxed with a bright gilt crescent rim with a lace strap, all embroidered in gold wire. The arm badges of rank and the tudor portcullis are in silver. An aiguillette of twisted gold gimp cord is fitted under the right shoulder epaulette and attached to the first button at the collar. The gold lace sash is $2\frac{1}{2}$ inches wide with three red stripes $\frac{1}{8}$ inch in width with a gilt clasp on the left side and round-headed tassels of gold and red twist to hang down 18 inches. The shoulder belt is $2\frac{1}{4}$ inches wide, of gold lace on a royal blue velvet ground. The pattern is an oakleaf design. The pouch is of blue velvet with the royal cypher and crown embroidered in gold wire. The pouch is edged in a 1-inch-wide gold lace. Only the captain, lieutenant and standard-bearer wear the gold aiguillette.

The sword belt is worn under the sash with gold lace sword slings on blue leather. The all-steel sword with a pierced hilt is the 1896 pattern introduced for all cavalry. The sword knot is of gold bullion with a lace strap. The tight fitting over-alls are of blue cloth with a broad gold lace stripe, $2\frac{1}{4}$ inches wide, down the outer seams. White gauntlet gloves are worn on all occasions, and the Gentlemen are armed with a long poled battle axe dating from the eighteenth century and covered in red velvet decorated with brass buttons. The blue cloak has a scarlet velvet collar and scarlet lining. A forage cap can be worn, of blue cloth with a scarlet band and a scarlet welt, and a leather peak embroidered in gold. The captains, on appointment, receive a gold Stick of Office from the sovereign. The lieutenant, standard bearer, the clerk of the cheque and the adjutant receive a silver stick. These are carried when on duty with the Corps. The sub-officer carries an ivory-headed stick which he receives from the captain upon appointment.

[PLATE 75

United States of America 1967

THIRD INFANTRY REGIMENT (THE OLD GUARD)

This is the oldest regular regiment of the infantry in the United States service, and serves as a Ceremonial Unit in Washington D.C. as the personal Escort for the President of the United States.

The regiment dates from 1784 and was then dressed in blue with red facings, white breeches, gaiters and waistcoat. The regiment served in the Mexican-American War with distinction at Cerro Gordo, Churubusco, and Chapultepec. In the American Civil War it served in the 2nd division. It is also the only regiment in the service of the U.S.A. which is permitted to use the shield of the United States as part of the regimental coat of arms.

The peaked cap is of blue cloth, on the top of which is an intertwined knot in gold cord. The peak is black leather with gold oak leaves for colonels. The cap badge is the U.S. eagle in relief with a group of stars above. The cap band is sky blue edged with gold piping. The chin strap is made of gold lace and the side buttons are gilt. The tunic is the dress blue uniform of the U.S. army, and is dark blue in colour, single-breasted and fastened by four gilt brass buttons depicting the American eagle. The lapels are decorated with the infantry crossed rifles. The officer's rank and arm of service is shown by the shoulder straps, these have gold-embroidered borders, enclosing the rank of the officer which is on a background of sky blue, the infantry colour. On each sleeve are two gold lace stripes $\frac{3}{4}$ inch apart, showing a sky blue light in between. Over the left shoulder passes a buff-coloured strap. By tradition this dates from the early days of the regiment when soldiers wore rawhide in the shoulder straps to distinguish themselves from other regiments. The twisted cord worn over the right arm is the mark of all infantry units in the U.S. army. White shirt and black tie are worn with this uniform. Around the waist is worn a sword belt of gold lace held by a gilt brass buckle depicting the American eagle and stars. The all-steel sword is carried hooked up on the left hip. The trousers are sky blue with a gold lace stripe $1\frac{1}{2}$ inches wide down the outer seams. Black shoes complete the uniform.

This unit also performs the duty of guarding the Unknown Soldier's Tomb. This is the oldest unit in the U.S. army and was an infantry regiment from 1784 to 1958 and an infantry battle group from 1958 to 1963. It now has special duties as a reinforced infantry battalion selected for its long and distinguished record.

The unit also has an Old Guard drum and fife corps dressed in eighteenth century uniform and is an integral part of the 3rd Infantry, the only one of its kind in the U.S. army.

75 United States of America – 3rd Infantry Regiment (Old Guard) 1967

76 Uruguay – Presidential Guard 1950

PLATE 76]

Uruguay 1950

PRESIDENTIAL GUARD

The President of Uruguay has as his Ceremonial Bodyguard the Regiment Blandengues Cavalry Number One. The Regiment was formed in 1797, but is titled after the national hero, Colonel Artigas, who in May 1811 defeated a large Spanish force at Las Piedras. His personal history was stormy; he became captain of a corps of the Spanish provincial service, but left in 1811 for the army of revolt. Later he formed a revolutionary army, but was outlawed by the Commander, Sarratea, for independent action. He then organised a troop of Grouchos, and this was so successful that by 1814 he was master of all Uruguay. He ejected the Portuguese from Montevideo and became Dictator. But he was ultimately defeated in 1820 and fled to Paraguay, from where he was sent in exile to Candelaria.

The uniform does not follow the usual German fashion of South America but is perhaps more reminiscent of the French style. The shako has a blue cloth body bound in black at the base and red at the top. The shako is decorated at the sides with chevron red stripes. The chin scales are brass, as is the shako plate depicting the arms of Uruguay. The short red plume is ball-shaped over a red tuft. Officers have a yellow ball with a red tuft, and the colonel an all-yellow plume.

The tunic is cut in a coatee style with tails, but is unusual in that it is worn open to display the waistcoat. It is blue in colour with red standing collar and red pointed cuffs. The turnbacks are red and the coat is also piped all round in red. The nine buttons are brass. Under the tunic, the waistcoat is of blue cloth, piped in red and brass buttoned. On each side of the coatee are two pockets, these also piped in red.

The riding breeches are of dark blue cloth with a red stripe along the outer seam and fastened with three brass buttons below the knee. The legs of the breeches fit into black riding boots which have half-laced tops that can be adjusted by the laces, which have ornamental tassels in black.

The brass stirrup-hilt sword has an all-steel scabbard. The saddlery is all white leather and the shabraque is of dark blue cloth edged in a gold lace with a red centre stripe. The shabraque is piped on the outer edge in red and embroidered in the corners with the arms of Uruguay, which is an oval shield surrounded by a wreath with a sun above. Uruguay has one other traditional regiment that wears a uniform of the 1820s complete with shakos and tail coats, and this is the Florida Infantry Battalion. It can be seen today so dressed on ceremonial occasions.

[PLATE 77

Venezuela 1820

PRESIDENTIAL GUARD

Simon Bolivar was the hero of South American Independence. He was born in Caracas, Venezuela. In 1812 he joined the insurgents at New Granada, but defeat forced him into exile. Undaunted, he tried again. In 1816 he drove all before him, becoming the hero of Liberation. The Spaniards were finally defeated at Carabobo in 1821 and Bolivar became President of Colombia, of which Venezuela was then a part. For the next two years, hard fighting succeeded in the formation of Independence for Equador and Peru, the upper part of this country changing its name to Bolivia in honour of the President. His adoption of dictatorial methods was justified by his position and the climate of opinion at that time and he was most successful in creating an independent South America.

This hussar guard regiment was founded by General Bolivar. Today, the President of Venezuela's Bodyguard is dressed in a similar fashion, except for the head-dress and the wearing of blue breeches. The 1820 uniform was greatly influenced by the British Napoleonic Wars; only the horse furniture and the barrel sash, in the Venezuelan national colours, betray its local origin.

The white fur busby carried on the right side a plain red cloth bag and a gilt cup at the front held a plain white feather plume. The head-dress was held to the head by means of a black leather chin strap. The dolman was of scarlet cloth with a standing collar of the same material. The dolman fastened down the centre by means of a row of eight brass buttons. The bars of lace across the chest ended in austrian knots at the outer end. Each was further decorated by a row of russia braid following around each bar. The collar was edged in a broad gold lace. The cuffs were plain red and carried austrian knot decorations. The white gauntlet gloves worn with a hussar uniform were another interesting variation. The seams of the dolman at the back were covered with a gold lace, an austrian knot to each at the shoulders. Over the left shoulder passed a white leather pouch belt with a black leather pouch. The straight bladed sword had a three-barred brass hilt with a plain steel scabbard with loose rings. The sword knot was a gold lace strap with a gold tassel. The barrel sash around the waist was in the national colours, the cords being blue, gold and red alternately.

Close-fitting red breeches were decorated at the thighs with elaborate austrian knots. The breeches fitted into black leather boots, the tops ornamented by gold lace binding and a gold tassel at the front. The spurs were white metal.

The horse harness was strongly influenced by Spanish style. The shabraque was a complete jaguar skin covering the saddle.

77 Venezuela – Presidential Guard 1820

78 Westphalia – Garde du Corps 1810

PLATE 78]

Westphalia 1810

GARDE DU CORPS

Jerome, King of Westphalia, was a brother of the Emperor Napoleon. The Kingdom of Westphalia had been carved out of the Rhine area with the town of Cassel as its capital. The king was rival to another Napoleonic dandy, King Joachim Murat. Jerome was married to Princess Catherine of Wurttemburg. At the ceremony the bride and groom were both in white, the groom's uniform rather more gold-embroidered than his bride's. Once, when wearing a satin coat and white plumed head-dress Jerome had been mistaken for the Empress Josephine.

A Garde du Corps was formed in 1810, dressed in the latest fashion. The Roman style helmet of gilt brass carried a white metal plate bearing a gilt shield surrounded by laurel leaves. On the shield was the king's monogram, and the brass ridge supported a black bearskin crest. On the left side a white hair plume sprang from a gilt cup. The chin strap of gilt overlapping plates was tied under the chin with a cord. The dark blue cloth tunic was single-breasted with a standing collar of red cloth embroidered with laurel leaves in gold wire. The round cuffs were also red and carried the same design. The cuirass was of steel, with brass studs around the edge. It was lined in red leather with a red velvet edge piped in gold. The straps were of overlapping plates on a red leather lining. In the centre was a silver shield bearing the king's monogram. The epaulettes were of gold with gold straps, crescents and bullions. A gold lace waist belt held the cuirass at the waist. The pouch belt was of gold lace on red morocco leather, a gilt shield displaying the royal monogram. From the right shoulder hung a gold cord aiguillette, fastened to the cuirass. The breeches were white buckskin and fitted into tall black leather jackboots. White gauntlet gloves were worn on mounted duties.

The sword belt was gold lace on red morocco leather. The sword had a gilt half-basket hilt, the cartouche displaying the king's monogram. The scabbard was steel with gilt mountings. The sword knot had a gold lace strap and gold tassel.

The shabraque was of blue cloth edged with two rows of gold lace, the pistol holsters were covered in the same manner with the addition of the royal crown and monogram embroidered in gold, the harness was black with gilt fittings and the reins were sewn with gold lace.

The Garde du Corps had been formed from volunteers who had fought with King Jerome in the Russian Campaign, before Napoleon had him returned from the front. They did not fire a shot in anger during their tenue as a Garde du Corps unit.

Jerome died in 1860, the last link with the old Empire; he was seventy-five. An incurable spendthrift, he had long since exhausted the fortune of his third wife, Marchesa Bartolini-Baldelli, and had to live on what he could borrow from his nephew, Napoleon III. Jerone was the only brother of Napoleon I to be photographed and was said to be very much like the first Emperor in physical features.

[PLATE 79

Württemburg 1860

LIFE GUARD

The last years of the House of Württemburg were clouded by the difficulties of finding an heir to the throne, the last king, William II, having only a daughter. Through morganatic marriages other branches had been eliminated, including the Duke of Teck, Queen Mary of Great Britain's father, and it looked as though the crown would pass to a Catholic branch of the family. However, the events of 1918 disposed of the problem.

The Kingdom of Württemburg, traditionally different in dress from the rest of the German nations, adopted a uniform with a hussar style head-dress similar in style to the French but without the bag. The chin scale, hooked up on the right-hand side, was more of an ornament, the cap being held on usually by a plain patent leather strap. The blue tunic was single-breasted with gilt brass buttons. Heavy gold corded epaulettes were slung from the right shoulder. The cap lines fastened to the top tunic button with tassels and flounders. The waist sash in full dress was rose red, hussar fashion, and the tassels hooked on to the front. The pouch belt was of gold lace and in the undress uniform was covered with a leather case fastened with buttons. The overalls were blue with rose red stripes along the outer seam. In undress or service loose leathered breeches were worn.

In undress the peaked cap was blue with rose red band and piping. The badges were a cockade of the national colours, red and black, with a gilt brass crown above. The troops' uniform was similar except in quality and the pouch belt and waist belt were of white leather. The men were armed also with lances carrying a rose red pennon.

The swords were curved, all steel with a steel three-barred hilt. Officers' sword knots had a leather strap with a gold bullion tassel.

The shabraque was blue, edged rose red, and in the lower corners carried the crown of Württemburg emboidered in rose red silks. The saddle roll was also blue piped in rose red with a crown in the centre of the same colour.

An earlier uniform, adopted soon after the Napoleonic Wars, was similar, the exception being the head-dress. This was a bell-topped shako shape, the 'bell' being much exaggerated. The body of the shako was covered in rose red cloth. The top was of heavy black leather; the bottom was bound in similar material and the peak was also of black leather. A gilt brass sunburst plate was emblazoned with the arms of Württemburg. Plaited gold cords hung across the front of the shako with a tassel on the left side, and on the right cords leading down to the tunic and fastened to the top button. From a cockade of the national colours, red and black, issued a double pom-pom of yellow, the top one cut to display a fringed end.

79 Württemburg – Life Guard 1860

80 Yugoslavia – Guard Cavalry 1937

PLATE 80]

Yugoslavia 1937

GUARD CAVALRY

The uniform of the Royal Guard of Yugoslavia was derived from units of the Serbian army. The red breeches were a feature of this cavalry before the First World War, when the uniforms adopted had been mainly Russian in character as in most of the Balkan States. The army at that time contained about three hundred thousand men.

Yugoslavia was created at the end of the First World War when Serbia, Croatia and Slovenia were united under one king, Peter I, previously King of Serbia. He was succeeded by his brother Alexander who was assassinated in 1934, at Marseilles. The new king, Peter II, ascended the throne at the age of eleven. The Regent, Prince Paul, favoured the German cause, but luckily a revolution in 1941 gave full powers to the king, who immediately joined the Allies. Outside the country a resistance was formed under General Mihailovitch. He was shot by the Communists, who seized power in 1946, not even allowing the King time to abdicate, nor allowing him his personal fortune.

The gala uniform for the Guard Cavalry consisted of a black lambskin cap with a madder-red bag and a white plume at the front. The cap was held to the head by a patent leather chin strap. The hussar dolman was green, ornamented with gold lace on the collar and cuffs and four rows of gold cord with gold buttons and drops. The pockets were also edged in gold. The plain light blue pelisse was edged in black fur. The pelisse had only two pockets – similar to the Austro-Hungarian fashion of the pre-First World War period. The riding breeches were madder red and fitted into gold-topped black riding boots.

The undress uniform consisted of a green peaked cap with a rosette of the national colours, red, blue and white. The green tunic had patch pockets, gold laced collar and cuffs, and the shoulder boards denoted the rank and regiment. The same type of riding breeches were used as for gala dress, but plain-topped boots were preferred for this order of uniform. Both uniforms were fastened with gold toggles, four in gala dress and six in undress.

The all steel sword had one ring and was suspended by a gold laced strap from under the tunic and carried a gold sword knot and acorn.

GLOSSARY

Adjutant	An officer who is appointed to assist the commanding officer of a regiment, or a staff officer
Aide-de-camp	A French word to denote an officer of the staff who passes on the orders of the commander
Aiguillette	Gold or silver plaited cords with metal points called aiglets, worn by ADCs, senior officers or regiment staffs, regiments of the Royal Household
Armour	See cuirass. The only metal armour to survive was the front plate, back plate and metal helmet usually adopted by gardes du corps
Atilla	German word for a dolman, the hussar frogged jacket
Austrian knot	Ornament in cord of two equal circles joined to one above, usually more elaborate as the rank increased
Bandolier	A leather belt to carry the ammunition pouches
Baton	A mark of supreme command in the field, now carried on ceremonial occasions by marshals
Bearskin	This has no resemblance to a busby which is an entirely different head-dress. A bearskin was adopted by grenadiers after the defeat of Napoleon. Many European States copied this head-dress which has been seen practically all around the world
Bell-top shako	Head-dress shaped as an up-turned bell, fashionable after Waterloo in most countries including the U.S.A.
Braid	Woven material in colours used to decorate soldiers uniforms
Breeches	Garment to cover the legs from waist to below the knee, buttoned at the sides. Worn with stockings
Brigandine	A style of body armour
Burnous	A cloak with a hood worn by Arabs and Moors
Cap lines	Cords fastened to the head-dress hanging loose and fastened around the collar to prevent loss if the head-dress came off in combat
Chasseurs	Light infantry
Chevron	Braid used to denote a non-commissioned rank. In some countries it was used to show length of service
Cockade	Rosette worn on a shako, usually to display the national colours. Usually made of pleated wool or silk or even painted metal
Cocked hat	Broad brimmed hat turned up each side, sometimes used as an undress headwear, later by field and staff officers
Comb	Ridge on top of a helmet
Counter epaulette	An epaulette without fringes
Cravat	Cloth worn around the neck, usually black, some gardes du corps used white
Crest	Fur covering to a comb or a badge plate on a head-dress
Cuirass	Armour of front and back plates used extensively by gardes du corps, made in steel or brass
Czapka	Polish head-dress which is quartered

Jazerant	Strips of metal sewn onto cloth or silk
Dolman	The short jacket or atilla worn by Hussar regiments usually frogged with cords. An elaborate and expensive part of hussar clothing
Dragoon	Line cavalry, capable of fighting on foot as well as mounted
Epaulette	A shoulder strap with a fringed end, originally a sign of rank
Facings	The collar, cuffs, turnbacks and plastrons of a uniform usually of a different colour to the rest of the coat
Field officer	Major, lieutenant-colonel, colonel
Flank companies	The light companies and grenadier companies of an infantry regiment
Flintlock	Musket fired by means of flint striking a steel which in turn ignites the powder
Forage cap	An undress cap worn on duties about the camp or when off duty. In the U.S.A. the term is used to denote a service cap
Fouraschka	A Russian field cap
Frock coat	A coat with skirts to the knees, double- or single-breasted. Usually worn as an undress item
Full dress	Gala or parade uniform
Fusil	Another term for flintlock
Fustinella	The pleated kilt worn by Greek Evzones
Gaiters	Leggings introduced in the eighteenth century, worn with breeches until *circa* 1840 when superseded by trousers, except in some guard units
Gauntlets	Gloves with stiff tops used by cavalry to protect their hands
Gorget	Metal plate to protect the throat and neck and later a stylised form for officer rank
Grenadier	Company within a regiment at one time armed with grenades and wearing a distinctive uniform, especially the mitre cap
Grenadier cap	Made of cloth and embroidered with devices, also decorated in fur. Later with metal front pieces
Hackle	Short plume on a head-dress
Halberd	Wooden shaft weapon with metal head, used by foot guards in ceremonial dress. In the eighteenth century used by sergeants
Helmet	Head-dress of metal used mainly by cavalry
Hessian boots	Knee boots with notched fronts fashionable in cavalry units
Hose	Lower leg garment
Hussar	Light cavalry, originally from Hungary, spread throughout the world, in dress characterised by the fur busby and pelisse
Kepi	Peaked cap, a low shako with a leather peak
Khaki	Persian word for dust-coloured, used originally by troops in India; a colour to merge with the surroundings, a camouflage
Kilt	Lower garment worn in Scotland, Ireland, Greece and other parts of Asia. Sometimes worn with trousers
Kittle	Russian tunic for summer wear

Kiva	Russian shako
Kurta	A plastron fronted tunic, originally Polish and worn by lancers
Lace	Braid used to decorate uniforms, woven with gold or silver thread on a silk base, or in plain colours for other ranks
Lancers	Horsemen armed with long spears, originally from Poland, and popular after the Napoleonic Wars in all parts of the world
Lapel	The turnback on a military coat usually of a different coloured cloth
Levee dress	Gala dress or full dress worn at palaces, festivities, balls and diplomatic receptions
Line regiment	Normal infantry regiments, not of the guard
Litewka	A form of greatcoat worn in the armies of the German States
Mirliton	Cavalry head-dress, conical in shape without a peak and wound around with a spiral of cloth with a tassel end
Musician	Bandsman in the army, often expected to act as stretcher bearer during a battle
Musket	Smooth bore fire-arm, usually flintlock
Overalls	Trousers that are tight fitting to the leg, usually strapped under the foot. In earlier periods they buttoned up at the sides
Pelisse	Hungarian horsemen used a wolfskin slung over the shoulders called a 'pelz', hence the word pelisse: in later days the inadequate greatcoat of the hussars, fur edged, but only coming to the waist, worn slung over the shoulders
Percussion gun	Weapon fired by a percussion cap being struck by the cock
Pickelhaube	Spiked helmet invented by the Russians and closely copied by the German States, especially Prussia
Plastron	Buttoned front of a coat usually associated with lancer regiments
Polrock	Frock coat with long skirts
Pom pom	Woollen ball tufts to decorate a shako, usually of various colours to denote the type of arm or regiment
Puttees	Cloth strips wound around the lower legs originally from India
Pugri	Cloth wound around an Indian cork helmet
Poshteen	Fur or sheepskin lined jacket worn in the Indian frontier Service
Queue	Eighteenth century name for hair tied at the back of the head in a black tube and covered by a black ribbon
Rank badge	Worn on the arm or shoulder strap
Reamer	Tool carried by artillerymen to clear the touch hole of a cannon
Regiment	Several companies comprise a regiment; usually one grenadier, centre and light companies
Rifle	Musket with a spiral grooved barrel: this helped in the accuracy of fire
Rosette	Circular ornament on the head-dress, often in material of wool or silk and in the national colours

Sabretache	Tache is the German word for pocket. This was an item hung by straps and used by cavalry to carry items such as maps etc. The flap was usually ornamented with a regimental crest or cypher
Saddlecloth	See shabraque
Sapper	Pioneer, engineer, used for trench digging and clearing gun positions and to 'sap' a trench towards an objective fortress
Sash	Item worn around the waist, usually to denote that the person is an officer, made of silk or woven gold and silver
Schapka	Alternative to lance cap
Shabraque	Saddlecloth, often ornamental with a laced edge and embroidered with crests on the tails
Shako	Peaked head-dress of leather or cloth
Shemagh	A head and face covering
Shoulder cords	Gold cord twisted or plaited and worn in place of epaulettes to denote officer rank
Shoulder straps	Used to hold the equipment or cross belts, often piped in a colour
Spatterdashes	Alternative to gaiters to save the legs from being spattered with mud or water
Spencer	A short jacket; term used in the U.S.A. for a tunic
Spontoon	Pole arm carried by officers, and later N.C.O.'s, to indicate rank
Sporran	Scottish Highlander's purse made of leather, occasionally fur covered
Stock	Worn around the neck, at first of black cloth and later leather, discarded in the 1850s
Superveste	Loose garment worn inside the palace by gardes du corps, often embroidered with crests
Swallows' nests	Shoulder ornaments used by bandsmen, most common in the German States to the present day
Sword knot	Strap worn on the sword to secure it to the hand in battle
Tjerkeska	Caucassian coat with cartridge fittings to the chest
Tricorne hat	Hat with three corners turned up
Trousers	Nether garments, usually loose fitting
Tunic	Sleeved coat reaching to above the knee; it followed on from the coatee
Turban	Indian head-dress or ornament, made of fur usually worn around the body of a helmet
Turnbacks	The coat tail linings pinned back
Uhlan	German word for lancer
Ulanka	German word for plastron-fronted lancer tunic
Undress	Uniform worn for working in and around the camp, similar to cavalry stable dress
Waist belt	Used to suspend a sword, bayonet or ammunition pouch, made of leather, or for officers, of gold/silver lace on a leather lining
Wings	Shoulder ornaments, the mark of flank companies, grenadiers or light infantry (jaeger), and sometimes bandsmen

BIBLIOGRAPHY

Uniformenkunde 18 vols Knotel 1890–1921

Handbuch der Uniformenkunde Knotel 1937

British Military Uniforms from contemporary sources W. Y. Carman HILL 1957

Indian Army Uniforms 2 vols W. Y. Carman HILL MORGAN-GRAMPIAN 1961

Uniforms des régiments Français de Louis XV à nous jours Paris 1945

The Russian army under Nicholas I 1825–55 N. C. Durham 1965

A history of the British army Fortesque London 1911

L'armée Russe sous le Tsar Alexander I Paris 1955

Military drawings and paintings in the collection of Her Majesty the Queen 2 vols PHAIDON
    1966–70

India's army D. Jackson SAMPSON LOW 1940

Famous fights of native Indian regiments R. Hodder HODDER & STOUGHTON 1914

Armies of India Lovette and McMunn A & C BLACK 1911

Durbar M. Merpes A & C BLACK 1903

Military uniforms in colour Kannick BLANDFORD 1961

Cavalry uniforms Wilkinson-Latham & Cassin-Scott BLANDFORD 1969

Infantry uniforms 2 vols Wilkinson-Latham & Cassin-Scott BLANDFORD 1970

Dix siècles de costume militaire Paris 1965 HATCHETTE

The anatomy of glory H. Brown LUND HUMPHRIES 1961

Historie universelle des armées 4 vols Paris 1966

History of the uniforms of the British army 5 vols London 1940–67

History of the uniforms of the British army 5 vols Cecil C. P. Lawson NORMAN MILITARY
    PUBLICATIONS London 1940–67

The armies of Europe Major-General G. McClellan 1861

British military uniforms Laver PENGUIN 1948

The history of the dress of the Royal Regiment of Artillery R. J. McDonald SOUTHERN & CO.
    1899

Les coiffures de l'armée Français Paris 1909

Der bunte Rock P. Martin SPRING BOOKS 1963

Vom Brustharnisch zum Waffenrock H. Schneider HUBER & CO. 1968

Le uniformi piu belle del mondo oggi 2 vols R. d'Ami AMZ 1966

The Queen's Guards H. Legge Bourke MACDONALD 1965

British yeomanry uniforms Simkin & Archer MULLER 1971

Fifty years of yeomanry uniform R. Harris MULLER 1972

Zolnierz Polski B Gembarzewski 4 vols Warsaw 1964

Great regiments V. Melegari WIEDENFELD & NICHOLSON 1969

L'Uniforme Italiana A. Gasparinetti EDIZIONI UNIVERSALI 1965

Les uniformes de l'Armée Français terre, mer, air M. Toussaint & E. Bucquoy 1935

Garde Impérial mamelukes R. & J. Brunon Marseille 1965

Battle dress F. Wilkinson GUINNESS 1970

The army in India 1850–1914 National Army Museum HUTCHINSON 1968

German army uniforms and insignia 1933–45 B. Davis ARMS & ARMOUR PRESS 1971

Helmets and head-dress of the Imperial Germany army 1870–1918 R. Rankin N. FLAYDERMAN
    1965

German military uniforms and insignia 1933–45 W E INC 1967

The Luftwaffe R. J. Bender BENDER INC 1972

Air organisation of the Third Reich R. J. Bender BENDER INC 1967

Records and badges of the British army Chichester & Short GALE & POLDEN 1900

Types of the Indian army F. Bremner BELL OF ARMS LTD 1964

Uniforms of the British army, navy and court T. Holding 1894

Illustrated histories of the Scottish regiments 3 vols P. Groves & H. Payne JOHNSTON LTD 1893

Pictorial history of the United States army G. Gurney CROWN 1966

Les Suisses au service étranger J. Bory NYON & CIE 1965

Die Preussische armee unter Friedrich Wilhelm II und Friedrich Wilhelm III 1786–1907
    P. Martin KELLER & CO. 1963

Die Preussische armee 1840–71 P. Martin KELLER & CO. 1970

Die Preussische armee 1808–39 P. Martin KELLER & CO. 1972

Die Französische armee 1789–1807 P. Martin KELLER & CO. 1969

The armies of today Brigadier-General Merritt 1893

Les régiments sous Louis XV Paris 1882

Die Oesterreichische armee 1700–1867 Vienna 1895

L'armée Russe, 1854 Lt.-Colonel Pajol Paris 1854

The book of the continental soldier H. Petersen STACKPOLE BOOKS 1968

Les vrais soldats de Napoléon L. Quennevat SEQUOIA-ELSEVIER 1968

Atlas de la Grand Armée L. Quennevat SEQUOIA-ELSEVIER 1966

L'armée Français, ses uniformes, son armament, son equipment Current series of plates Paris

French army regiments and uniforms W. Thorburn ARMS & ARMOUR PRESS 1969

Soldiers of the American army F. P. Todd New York 1941

Historical description of the uniforms and armaments of the Russian army 30 vols St. Petersburg
    1844–56

L'armée Russe 3 vols W. Zueguintzow PRIVATELY 1969

Military fashion J. Mollo BARRIE & JENKINS 1972

Album de guide des uniformes de l'Armée Français 1780–1848 H. Malibran Paris 1907

Formations und uniformierunggeschichte des Preussischen Heeres 1808–1914 2 vols Paul Pietsch
    SCHULZ 1966

Les uniformes de l'Armée Français 1872–1914 8 vols GALOT & ROBERT

Germany army, navy uniforms and insignia 1871–1918 E. Hoffschmidt & W. Tantum
    W.E. INC 1968

Historie de l'Armée Français General Weygard FLAMMARION 1961

La Seconde Guerre Mondiale 2 vols R. Cartier PARIS MATCH

The age of Napoleon M. Davidson & J. Herold HORIZON 1963

Cronica del Trafe militar en Mexico del Siglo XVI al XX J. Hefter 1955

The life of Napoleon Bonaparte 4 vols W. Sloane MACMILLAN 1894

History of the regiments of the British army Major R. Barnes SEELEY SERVICE 1950

The British army of 1914 Major R. Barnes SEELEY SERVICE 1968

The soldiers of London Major R. Barnes SEELEY SERVICE 1963

Military uniforms of Britain and the Empire Major R. Barnes SEELEY SERVICE 1960

The uniforms and history of the Scottish regiments Major R. Barnes SEELEY SERVICE 1960

Hertzogin Viktoria Luis W. Germany 1969

Uniforms of the United States army 2 vols H. Ogden GOTTINGER VERLAGSANSTALT 1907

Uniformi militari Italiane 2 vols V. Delguidice BRAMANTE 1968

Album militaire BOUSSARD VALADON & CIE Paris 1890

The ancient art of warfare 2 vols J. Boudet BARRIE & ROCKLIFF 1966

Uniforms of the SS 6 vols Andrew Mollo HISTORICAL RESEARCH UNIT
De Nederlandse cavalerie P. Forbes Wels C. VAN DISHOECK 1963
De Nederlandse infanterie H. Ringoir C. VAN DISHOECK 1968
Napoleon O. Aubry HAMLYN 1964
Deutchlands Ruhmeshalle H. Muller-Bohn 1937
Autour du drapeau 1789–1899 General Thoumas Paris 1890

TABLE OF PLATES

The description appears on the back of each plate

39 Libya – Royal Guard 1951
40 Mexico – Imperial Palace Guard 1865
41 Modena – Mounted Bodyguard 1753
42 Monaco – Palace Guard 1970
43 Montenegro – Royal Escort 1900
44 Morocco – Halberdier of the Guard 1973
45 Kingdom of Naples – Guard 1852
46 Nepal – Foot Guards 1970
47 Netherlands – Foot Guards 1752
48 Nigeria – Presidential Mounted Guard 1970
49 Norway – His Majesty's Royal Guard 1970
50 Panama – Presidential & National Guard 1970
51 Parma – Grenadiers of the Guard 1853
52 Peru – Presidential Guard Cuirassiers 1960
53 Philippine Islands – Governor's Bodyguard 1896
54 Poland – King's Bodyguard 1786
55 Portugal – Mounted Royal Guard 1905
56 Prussia – Garde du Corps 1843
57 Rome – The Noble Guard 1970
58 Rumania – Royal Escort 1927
59 Russia – Pavlowsky Grenadier Guards 1830
60 Russia – Cuirassier Empress Chevalier Guards 1862
61 Sardinia – Grenadier Guards 1848
62 Saxe Gotha – Garde du Corps 1758
63 Saxony – Garde du Corps 1811
64 Scotland – Bodyguard for Scotland 1911
65 Senegal – Presidential Guard Gendarmerie 1970
66 Sikkim – Royal Bodyguard 1970
67 South Africa – Presidential Guard 1969
68 Spain – Albarderos 1896
69 Sudan – Presidential Guard 1969
70 Sweden – Life Guards 1807
71 Thailand – Royal Palace Guard 1970
72 Tunisia – Spahis of the Guard 1970
73 Turkey – Interior Guard Beylerbey Palace 1854
74 United Kingdom – The Honourable Corps of Gentlemen at Arms 1970
75 United States of America – 3rd Infantry Regiment (Old Guard) 1967
76 Uruguay – Presidential Guard 1950
77 Venezuela – Presidential Guard 1820
78 Westphalia – Garde du Corps 1810
79 Württemburg – Life Guard 1860
80 Yugoslavia – Guard Cavalry 1937